ETpedia™

Pronunciation

500 ideas and activities for teaching pronunciation

Intonation

θ

i:

ʊ

dʒ

phonemes

diphthongs

segmental features

æ

John Hughes and Gerhard Erasmus

Series editor: John Hughes

www.myetpedia.com

ETpedia Pronunciation

500 ideas and activities for teaching pronunciation

Published by:

Pavilion Publishing and Media Ltd
Blue Sky Offices Shoreham
25 Cecil Pashley Way
Shoreham-by-Sea BN43 5FF
UK

Tel: 01273 434 943
Email: info@pavpub.com
Web: www.pavpub.com

First published 2022.

A catalogue record for this book is available from the British Library.

Print: 978-1-914010-87-3
Epub: 978-1-914010-88-0
PDF ebook: 978-1-914010-89-7
Kindle: 978-1-914010-90-3

Acknowledgements

The author and publisher are grateful to those who have given permissions to reproduce the following illustrations.

Illustration credits: page 66: Sandy Millin. Reproduced with kind permission; page 100: Jon Hird. Reproduced with kind permission.

Note: We respect all registered trademarks: all website domain names, site names, software brand names, screenshots and extracts from software products are © by the website owner or publisher named.

Pavilion is the leading training and development provider and publisher in the health, social care and allied fields, providing a range of innovative training solutions underpinned by sound research and professional values. We aim to put our customers first, through excellent customer service and value.

Authors: John Hughes and Gerhard Erasmus
Glossary author: Kirsten Holt
Development editor: Penny Hands
Production editor: Hannah Hobbs, Pavilion Publishing and Media Ltd
Publishing head: Kirsten Holt, Pavilion Publishing and Media Ltd
Cover design: Emma Dawe, Pavilion Publishing and Media Ltd
Page layout and typesetting: Emma Dawe, Pavilion Publishing and Media Ltd
Printing: CMP (UK) Ltd

ETpedia Pronunciation

500 ideas and activities for teaching pronunciation

Also available from Pavilion ELT at Pavilion Publishing and Media

A Comprehensive Language Coaching Handbook	ISBN 978-1-80388-035-8
An Introduction to Evidence-Based Teaching in the English Language Classroom	ISBN 978-1-913414-89-4
A Practical Introduction to Teacher Training in ELT	ISBN 978-1-910366-99-8
Become an Online English Teacher	ISBN 978-1-910366-77-6
Best Practices for Blended Learning	ISBN 978-1-911028-84-0
Integrating Authentic Listening into the Language Classroom	ISBN 978-1-914010-45-3
Learning While Teaching	ISBN 978-1-914010-37-8
Live Online Teaching	ISBN 978-1-914010-41-5
Putting the Human Centre Stage	ISBN 978-1-912755-28-8
Structuring Fun for Young Learners in the ELT Classroom	ISBN 978-1-913414-53-5
Structuring Fun for Young Language Learners Online	ISBN 978-1-913414-85-6
Teaching and Learning English in the Early Years	ISBN 978-1-80388-039-6
Teaching English One to One 2nd Edition	ISBN 978-1-912755-66-0
Teaching English with Drama	ISBN 978-1-898789-11-6
Teaching Grammar: From Rules to Reasons	ISBN 978-1-911028-22-2
The Creative Teacher's Compendium	ISBN 978-1-913414-52-8
Understanding Teenagers in the ELT Classroom	ISBN 978-1-912755-00-4
Understanding Teenage Language Learners Online	ISBN 978-1-914010-33-0
ETpedia	ISBN 978-1-910366-13-4
ETpedia Business English	ISBN 978-1-911028-20-8
ETpedia Exams	ISBN 978-1-911028-80-2
ETpedia Grammar	ISBN 978-1-912755-02-8
ETpedia Management	ISBN 978-1-912755-27-1
ETpedia Materials Writing	ISBN 978-1-911028-62-8
ETpedia Teacher Training	ISBN 978-1-913414-16-0
ETpedia Technology	ISBN 978-1-911028-58-1
ETpedia Teenagers	ISBN 978-1-911028-44-4
ETpedia Vocabulary	ISBN 978-1-912755-26-4
ETpedia Young Learners	ISBN 978-1-911028-21-5
Successful International Communication	ISBN 978-1-912755-13-4
Teaching English to Health and Social Care Workers	ISBN 978-1-911028-07-9

For full details of all our books, events and our new-look *Modern English Teacher* magazines, go to: **https://www.pavpub.com/pavilion-elt**.

Visit: **www.modernenglishteacher.com**

Contents

Introduction

10 reasons for using this resource 8

10 ways to use this resource 10

10 facts about the authors 12

Section 1: Getting started

Unit 1: 10 reasons to include pronunciation in all your lessons 14

Unit 2: 10 reasons why pronunciation isn't taught in lessons................................. 16

Unit 3: 10 questions to ask yourself when planning lessons 18

Unit 4: 10 ways to identify your students' pronunciation needs 20

Unit 5: 10 pairs of pronunciation-related terms 22

Section 2: The basic toolkit

Unit 6: 10 tools and resources... 26

Unit 7: 10 tips on using your voice... 29

Unit 8: 10 ways to vary your pronunciation drills 31

Unit 9: 10 articulators of speech 34

Unit 10: 10 questions about mouth positions 36

Unit 11: 10 uses of the whole body 38

Unit 12: 10 tips on using your board or screen... 40

Section 3: Knowledge and problem solving

Unit 13: 10 things to know about word stress... 44

Unit 14: 10 tips for presenting word stress 46

Unit 15: 10 activities for practising word stress.. 48

Unit 16: 10 things to know about sentence stress 51

Unit 17: 10 activities for practising sentence stress 53

Unit 18: 10 things to know about individual sounds....................................... 56

Unit 19: 10 activities for practising individual sounds..................................... 59

Unit 20: 10 reasons why learners have problems with individual sounds 62

Unit 21: 10 key terms for describing and presenting connected speech 65

Unit 22: 10 ways to introduce and practise connected speech 67

Unit 23: 10 things to know and consider about intonation................................. 71

Unit 24: 10 activities to present and practise intonation.................................. 74

Section 4: Integrating pronunciation

Unit 25: 10 ways to integrate more pronunciation into your lesson planning 78

Unit 26: 10 ways to integrate pronunciation with the tenses 81

Unit 27: 10 ways to integrate pronunciation with grammar 85

Unit 28: 10 tendencies and activities for asking questions 88

Unit 29: 10 ways to integrate pronunciation with vocabulary 91

Unit 30: 10 ideas for homophones and homographs 94

Unit 31: 10 ideas for integrating pronunciation into listening lessons 97

Unit 32: 10 ways to integrate pronunciation into reading lessons 100

Unit 33: 10 ways to help with sound and spelling.. 102

Unit 34: 10 activities for spelling aloud 105

Unit 35: 10 steps for improving the delivery of a presentation............................. 108

Unit 36: 10 ideas for integrating correction 111

Unit 37: 10 tips for teaching pronunciation to young learners 113

Section 5: Online teaching and technology

Unit 38: 10 tips for teaching pronunciation with a video-conferencing platform ... 118

Unit 39: 10 benefits of online pronunciation teaching.. 121

Unit 40: 10 reasons for using technology.. 123

Unit 41: 10 ways of incorporating technology 125

Unit 42: 10 questions about recording students' voices.. 127

Unit 43: 10 websites and tools to incorporate in pronunciation teaching 129

Section 6: Materials writing and professional development

Unit 44: 10 pronunciation in a coursebook questions to consider.......................... 132

Unit 45: 10 types of activities for writing pronunciation materials 133

Unit 46: 10 tips on scripting and recording pronunciation materials 137

Unit 47: 10 types of interactive activities for pronunciation materials 140

Unit 48: 10 pronunciation questions to consider 142

Unit 49: 10 tips for continuing professional development...................................... 145

Unit 50: 10 more recommended books to read and refer to................................... 147

Appendix 149

Glossary 180

Introduction

10 reasons for using this resource

Introduction

1. Everything in one place

ETpedia Pronunciation brings together a collection of key terms and information, ideas, tips and classroom activities for a one-stop, quick and easy reference. It's organised into 50 units with 10 ideas in each unit. You will find the key terms are written in bold within the units, signaling they can be found in the glossary on pages 180–186.

2. Range of contexts

This book does more than provide classroom ideas: it aims to help teachers better understand different approaches and methods of teaching pronunciation and how to adapt to any given context and the learners' needs.

3. You're new to teaching or in need of some new ideas

If you are new to teaching, this resource will be invaluable in supporting you on your way. If you've been teaching for a while, this resource might both remind you of techniques and activities you haven't used in a while and offer you fresh new ideas to increase your repertoire.

4. Supplement your coursebook

Many teachers find that their coursebook doesn't provide enough input and practice with pronunciation, so they need to supplement it. You'll find plenty of ideas in this book that help you meet the needs of your students in creative ways to support their English pronunciation development, in and out of class.

5. You read on the run

Teachers who need something bite-sized that they can dip into between classes will appreciate the format of the book.

6. You want something that works

The ideas in the book are designed to be simple, effective and down-to-earth.

7. You haven't got much time to prepare lessons

Most of the practical ideas and activities in this book are straightforward and need little or no preparation. In addition to these ideas and activities, you will also find a bank of easy-to-use photocopiable worksheets in the appendix. These relate to the units, and can be photocopied for use in your teaching context. Photocopiable worksheets are indicated in the text by this symbol:

8. Teacher's block

You might be familiar with the term 'writer's block' in relation to novelists. However, there are also times when teachers simply cannot come up with original ideas or activities for students. Keep this resource book in the staffroom for such moments and open it on any page. Maybe one of the ten tips on that page will give you a new idea for teaching pronunciation.

9. You're looking for staffroom discussion-starters

Senior teachers and heads of department can select units of the book to kick-start staffroom conversations, peer collaboration and idea-sharing among colleagues. Use the activities marked with the CPD symbol 🗣 in teacher development/inset sessions. Read a unit, or one of the quotes from experts in the field in the book, and then discuss it with your colleagues. Share your own ideas and techniques.

10. You enjoy teaching

This book is written for teachers who love teaching, and who want their lessons to be memorable and enjoyable – both for their students and themselves.

"I frequently use the ideas in ETpedia as a kind of checklist when preparing my lessons."

Mario Lecluyze, teacher and trainer, Belgium

Introduction

10 ways to use this resource

This resource has been written for English language teachers who would like to develop their pronunciation teaching skills in both face-to-face and online lessons. It can be read and used in different ways according to your needs, interests and level of experience.

1. Cover to cover

If you are less confident at teaching pronunciation or are adapting to a new teaching context, you might be using this resource as a way to develop your teaching technique. If so, it's worth reading the book from cover to cover in order to get a thorough overview and grounding in the theory and practice of teaching pronunciation.

As you make your way through this book, compile a 'Top 50' by circling the point that you like the most in the unit when you get to the end of each unit. Then add notes about how you used it in class and how the students reacted. When you finish the book, you'll have a list of your 50 favourite activities to use in class.

2. Read a section

The contents (pages 5–6) will direct you to different sections, with groups of units on a specific aspect of vocabulary pronunciation. Some sections may not be immediately relevant to the students you are working with, or to the resources you have available, so you can ignore them for now. Other sections will be of immediate relevance and will provide you with key information and ideas to plan effectively and teach pronunciation to your students.

3. Finding the pronunciation point you need

This book can be dipped into when planning practical activities for lessons. Within many of the units, which are listed in the contents (pages 5–6), you'll find the pronunciation point you need and related activities. The first section of the book also provides you with the background knowledge you need for understanding how pronunciation works. So, you can choose to approach the units in whatever order best suits the needs of you and your learners.

4. Planning a lesson

Every unit provides you with 10 different ideas and activities. You might be looking for a single activity to supplement your coursebook or you may want to revise the pronunciation studied in the previous lesson. You'll find a short introduction to the pronunciation with information on when it's normally taught and why it's used.

Read the unit critically – no two language classes are the same, and experiences differ. Modify and adapt ideas to suit your own needs.

5. Teaching online

Perhaps you have recently started teaching live classes online and need help with the challenge of teaching pronunciation via platforms such as Zoom or Microsoft Teams (or equivalent). If so, jump straight to the section in the book with tips and ideas for teaching pronunciation online.

6. Photocopiable activities

Look out for the photocopiable icon when you read the 500 ideas. This means that in the appendix you'll find a ready-to-use photocopiable sheet that supports the activity.

7. Suggestions for homework and self-study

You'll find throughout the book suggested tasks for students to do after the lesson on their own. Rather than provide you with a typical homework activity, such as completing a gapfill exercise (which you can find in lots of other books), it suggests a motivating task such as noticing how the phonological feature works in real-life contexts, or gives suggestions of how learners can practise out of class for you to review and be able to give feedback on later.

8. Activities and reflective tasks

This icon denotes an activity or reflective task that will help you develop your own style of teaching pronunciation and encourages experiential learning. Activities can be done individually or collectively with fellow teachers. They will not only focus your mind on your learning through this book, but also help you understand what works best and why for your learners.

9. Revisit ideas

Not all ideas work for every class, and you don't teach the same level or type of class all the time. Go back to ideas you've used before and weigh up if they will work with your next set of students. Use this book as a notebook to jot down ideas of what you can use with your new class and then how it impacted their learning.

10. Common difficulties

Many units give tips relating to the difficulties students can have with the pronunciation point in question. Some of the units also highlight the way a student's first language might impact on their English pronunciation, or the reasons why students can get confused about what they hear or say. Add your own notes about any additional difficulties you encounter with your students. You may then want to share these with other teachers in your institution to discuss the best ideas and techniques to help your students.

"ETpedia saves hours of planning time and opens opportunities for variation, adaptation and even creating my own materials inspired by the ideas it offers."

Ayat Al-Tawal, teacher, Egypt

10 facts about the authors

Gerhard Erasmus and John Hughes have over 50 years' experience of teaching and teacher training between them.

Gerhard Erasmus ...

▶ has been living in Taiwan since 2003 and is married with three children.

▶ trains on the Cambridge DELTA, Trinity Diploma, and Trinity TYLEC, and is keen on finding innovative ways of dealing with and practising pronunciation in the classroom.

▶ worked as a professional magician during his university years and still occasionally incorporates magic into training and teaching. He came third in the Taiwan close-up magic championships in 2006.

▶ enjoys writing and presenting, but enjoys few things more than sitting down with a teacher and doing one-to-one development work.

▶ loves walking his dog at night as it gives him time to think, reflect and plan.

John Hughes ...

▶ remembers teaching his very first English pronunciation lesson in Poland in 1993. He taught word stress – very nervously!

▶ wrote the very first ETpedia resource book for teachers, published in 2014, and is the series editor for the many ETpedia titles which have followed.

▶ has trained teachers from all over the world and prepared many teachers for the Trinity DipTESOL qualification with its phonology interview.

▶ is a coursebook author, and has written more than 50 published titles for students and teachers.

▶ has an author site at www.johnhugheselt.com.

Introduction

Section 1:
Getting started

Most sections and units of this book contain practical activities to help you teach different aspects of pronunciation or how to best incorporate it within your lessons effectively. But in order to start teaching pronunciation, a teacher should understand the value and role pronunciation can play in learning, reasons why it may not be covered in course material and how to plan using pronunciation in lessons. In this introductory section, Units 1, 2 and 3 will provide you with that knowledge. These units set the scene and aim to highlight the valuable role teaching pronunciation plays in successful learning.

Units 4–5 in this section move on to looking at learners' needs and common phonological features you are likely to cover in your everyday lessons. The aim of Unit 4 is to make sure you can identify your students' pronunciation needs early on so you can support them in future lessons and ensures their learning with you gets off to a good start. Unit 5 provides a list of common phonology terminology that sound similar and can be confused to ensure you understand key terminology before moving on the rest of this book. Note that many of the words in this unit will be re-used and expanded upon throughout the rest of the book so it's useful to check your understanding beforehand.

If you are new to teaching, it's probably wise to start by reading these five units straight away. If you already have some experience as a teacher, you might be familiar with many of the concepts and terms; if so, just skim through and check any you haven't met before or that you've forgotten.

10 reasons to include pronunciation in all your lessons

Unit 1

When we think about language lessons, we generally think about either the skills: reading, listening, writing, and speaking, or the most popular systems: grammar and vocabulary. While there is a lot of interaction between skills and systems, pronunciation is often only focused on in speaking lessons, even though it has a very important effect on all the skills and how grammar and vocabulary is recalled.

1. Language is stored in sound bites

When you think of a word, your brain activates the sound. This sound is related to your understanding of the word, whether that be an image of an item (for example, a tree) or just an understanding of the word (for example, happiness). If we don't focus on pronunciation when we teach, students cannot effectively store the language in their brains and therefore cannot recall it effectively.

2. Pronunciation is different from linguistic knowledge

Pronunciation is a physical skill. It requires muscle memory; the muscles and organs responsible for producing the sound cannot do so simply by our thinking about it. To create a memory of how to produce the sound, our tongue, lips, vocal cords, lungs, and everything else responsible for producing the sounds rely on regular practice. Not focusing on pronunciation means students never develop this muscle memory.

3. Pronunciation in speaking creates confidence

Learning a foreign language can be intimidating. One area that can be automated, meaning there is no need to consciously think about it, is the pronunciation of words, chunks and common patterns. If students are confident about how to pronounce chunks and words, they are a lot more likely to use them in speaking. And the more often they use them in speaking, the more likely they are to feel confident enough to experiment with new words and chunks.

4. Pronunciation in listening supports decoding

If you have ever listened to someone speaking a completely foreign language, it probably sounded like a continuous stream of sounds. There is no indication where one words starts and the next one begins. Combining lexical and grammatical knowledge, pronunciation allows students to identify word boundaries, as well as key lexical and grammatical items, and to activate lexical and syntactical priming. Priming makes it much easier to predict accurately what is coming next in the text or spoken utterances they are listening to.

5. Pronunciation in reading supports understanding

Most, if not every, reader has a 'voice inside their head' when they read. This voice inside your head is not only reaffirmation that language is stored in sound bites, but also reflects how we read, especially when we read for details. Actually turning off the voice in your head is one of the key techniques to use when you want to increase your reading speed or develop better skimming and scanning skills in reading.

6. Pronunciation supports writing

Despite the common sentiment that English spelling is very confusing and it is pointless remembering rules, a large percentage of words do actually adhere to very simple rules. While English does contain some common words that don't follow the rules (for instance, *have*, which is pronounced **hav**, not **heɪv**), the majority of words are actually pronounced in a predictable way based on spelling. A lot of spelling rules are actually based on pronunciation rules, so it is often a good idea to sound a word out when you want to write it.

7. Pronunciation accelerates writing and reading

Reading and writing are literacy skills, but when we read, we notice the letters and words and convert these to sounds in our heads through a process called **subvocalisation**. You might even sometimes find your lips or your throat moving when you are reading in your head. Similarly, when we are reading over what you have written or thinking about what you are going to write, we often think about what it will sound like first. Therefore, a clear focus on pronunciation, even in writing and reading lessons, allows for much faster decoding of written language and much more effective writing.

8. Pronunciation and vocabulary

There are various levels of 'knowing a word', and while meaning should always come first, pronunciation of the word comes a close second. Next, students should focus on the pronunciation of the word within common collocations. Ensure that students are aware of the individual sounds that make up the word, the word stress and the unstressed syllables, as well as how the word sounds in connected speech.

9. Pronunciation and grammar

When we look at grammar purely as patterns in the language, it becomes obvious that certain patterns highlight certain pronunciation features. These could include intonation, tonic stress, weak forms, rhythm and stress, connected speech (especially between content words and function words) and a range of other areas of pronunciation that could be highlighted and developed (see Unit 27, pages 85–87). How often in classes do we look at tenses and the related question forms, but not highlight the difference in intonation?

10. Students want to focus on pronunciation

This last tip is potentially the most important one. Students want to work on pronunciation because they know they will find themselves in situations where they want to use certain words or patterns, but they are unsure how to pronounce them. This does not mean they want to sound like someone whose first language is English; rather, they want to speak with confidence, and they want to be familiar enough with the phonology of the language to be able to decode other people's speech.

Unit 1

10 reasons why pronunciation isn't taught in lessons

Unit 1 (pages 14–15) looked at reasons why we should teach pronunciation in our classrooms. In contrast, it's also helpful to recognise why teachers sometimes avoid including it in their lessons. Perhaps you will even recognise that you have given these reasons for not integrating pronunciation into your classes yourself. By addressing them early on in this book, we can start to consider how we might counter such reasoning.

1. It's perceived as difficult

When people talk about pronunciation, they often use specialised terms (see Unit 5, pages 22–23). For this reason, pronunciation can be perceived as difficult. And yet, we accept – and in some cases embrace – the same level of terminology when talking about grammar. Teachers are often unfamiliar with ways of talking about pronunciation. Fortunately, if you are one of those teachers, the fact you are now looking at this book suggests you are keen to address this.

2. It is physical

Unlike teaching other aspects of English, teaching pronunciation is primarily physical. Students need to use their jaw, lips and tongue to produce sounds they have never had to produce before. In fact, the speech habits from the student's first language might never disappear. In general, having an accent isn't a problem but difficulty in producing new sounds may affect intelligibility. So a pronunciation teacher becomes like a physical trainer trying to get the students to exercise and train parts of their body. As anyone who has been to the gym or taken part in sporting activities knows, this is challenging to do and takes repeated periods of time.

3. Not enough time

All teachers face the pressure of time in their lessons; we often feel that we have to get through the syllabus, get through the coursebook, or get everyone ready for the end-of-term test or exam. As a result, we tend to prioritise things like grammar and vocabulary over pronunciation. However, pronunciation often benefits from a little and often approach in the classroom, so try to integrate it at least once into every lesson, even if it's just one aspect for one or two minutes.

4. An individual problem

When teaching classes made up of students with different first languages, pronunciation issues often relate to a particular individual. For instance, one student might say a sentence that sounds like 'I feel right' when they mean 'I feel light'. In such a case, the teacher might deal with their difficulty with the phonemes **l** and **r** individually and on the spot rather than teach it to the whole class.

5. Washback from tests and exams

The majority of tests and exams focus on testing grammar and vocabulary or some of the four skills. Arguably, exams such as the international Cambridge ESOL or IELTS exams test pronunciation indirectly through inclusion of a speaking paper and a listening paper. However, pronunciation is not explicitly tested, and therefore not taught so much. However, marks are given indirectly for pronunciation in such exams, so improving pronunciation can improve a grade.

6. Harder to plan for

When planning a lesson, there is a tendency to plan the lesson aims around a grammar point, a set of vocabulary, or a reading or listening comprehension task. We rarely plan a whole lesson around a single pronunciation point such as word stress.

7. Phonemic script is time-consuming to learn and use

The fact that English has 26 letters but 44 sounds does not work in its favour from the point of view of the student! The 44 sounds are represented by phonemic symbols and words can be written in phonemic script. Not surprisingly, having learned how to read and write English with the 26 letters of the alphabet, many students are not keen to then learn a second type of script with 44 phonemes. In the past, a teacher could explain the value of knowing phonemic script by pointing out that print-based dictionaries provided the phonemic transcription of a word so that a learner could work out how to say it. But nowadays, as so many students have electronic dictionaries which will play an audio recording of a word, many people question the need for students to know phonemic script.

8. Which pronunciation are we teaching?

In recent years there has been a debate over what standard of pronunciation we are teaching. Typically, language schools that claim to teach 'British English' base pronunciation around a standard pronunciation in which students listen to a version of pronunciation originating in the south-east of England among the middle classes. Of course, in reality, British English consists of many regional accents. Similarly, the standard pronunciation of 'American English' reflects the accent of one region, ignoring the many others. This British English/American English dichotomy still prevails in language schools, when in fact there is no standard English. Because English is a global language, every speaker should aim for intelligible pronunciation and teachers should regard their own accent as a standard for students to aim for in class.

9. Nothing beyond just drilling

There is a perception that teaching pronunciation is about providing a model of the target pronunciation (either from the teacher or on a recording) and then having students repeat it. While this kind of drilling is an important aspect of pronunciation teaching, there are many other ways to present and practise it – as this book aims to demonstrate. It's also this perception that leads to a belief that listening to and producing pronunciation is something students can do on their own at home and that time in class can be better spent on other things. However, it ignores the need for teachers to actively help with areas such as manner and place of articulation or to draw attention to features of connected speech in a listening which, on their own, students are unlikely to notice.

10. Teacher training courses

Many training courses do not include much guidance on how to teach pronunciation. Often, a training course might only consist of one or two sessions on pronunciation in which a few 'fun' activities are presented to use in class. In other words, pronunciation is not presented as something to be taught systematically and regularly in the same way that grammar or vocabulary often are. If you are a teacher trainer reading this book, we hope you will find that it helps you to place greater emphasis on pronunciation on your courses.

Unit 2

10 questions to ask yourself when planning lessons

It can be difficult to decide which features of pronunciation to focus on in your lessons. While it is easy to be guided by the language that is presented in the coursebook, these ten tips should help you think beyond the coursebook and increase the variety and depth of pronunciation teaching in your lessons.

1. Does the same pronunciation feature exist in the students' L1?

The effect of **L1 interference** can be predicted if we know which sounds exist or do not exist in a learner's first language (L1). In classes where students have different L1s, certain sounds might be problematic for some learners but not for others. Being aware of sounds that exist in learners' L1 means that pronunciation lessons or activities on individual sounds can be much more focused and useful.

2. Is it productive or receptive?

When you plan your pronunciation aim, consider whether your main focus is on learners producing the pronunciation or only on recognising a pronunciation feature. For example, you might need learners to be able to produce a certain phoneme (see Unit 18, pages 56–58) in order to make a word intelligible when they speak, but they may only need to recognise, for example, a feature of connected speech (see Units 21–22, pages 65–70) in order to understand an authentic listening text.

3. How much time do I have in my lesson to focus on it?

This aspect of planning can be the most frustrating for teachers. We want our students to achieve, to improve, and to enjoy the learning journey, but we only have so much time. The other issue that complicates how we plan pronunciation is that it is often integrated into other stages. As a rule of thumb, it is good to assign ten percent of your lesson time (at least five minutes of a 50-minute lesson) to focus on pronunciation practice.

4. Does the pronunciation issue affect intelligibility or not?

Intelligibility affects both how we plan pronunciation and how we approach error correction. This does not mean that we should avoid areas that do not affect intelligibility, but rather that we should focus first and foremost on issues that do. It is likely that there will be a range of pronunciation issues in a specific class and at different levels. By prioritising issues that affect intelligibility, we are helping our learners address immediate issues and ensuring that they can confidently communicate with other speakers using English.

5. Am I going to use phonemic script?

While there are lots of arguments for and against using **phonemic script**, it would be good to consider if the use of phonemic script might help learners notice and become more aware of possible pronunciation issues. This is particularly relevant when sounds change in connected speech, or when you are focusing on individual sounds. For example, when highlighting the pronunciation of the word *rose*, it might be easy to say it is pronounced in a similar way to *nose*. Students might, however, be mispronouncing *nose* **nəʊz** as **nəʊs**. Highlighting the pronunciation of the final sound using phonemic script might be very useful, and should therefore always be considered when planning pronunciation lessons. It is also particularly useful to highlight unstressed syllables using phonemic script.

Unit 3

6. Do students understand the meaning of the words or sentences I am going to focus on?

It is important to ensure that pronunciation practice does not happen in a vacuum. Ensuring that students understand the meaning of the words and sentences before focusing on their pronunciation increases the likelihood of their using the words and sentences later on. When planning a pronunciation stage, be sure to either use words or sentences that your learners are already familiar with, or to plan for a meaning-focused stage before the pronunciation stage.

7. How will I introduce the pronunciation?

Once you have decided on the pronunciation points you want to focus on, try to find a recording that models them. If you want to focus on something receptive, consider using a recording of authentic speech, which students have to decode. If the aim is productive pronunciation, you might need to model it yourself or use a specially made recording (for example, the type of recording you find in a coursebook).

8. How will I make the pronunciation focus learner-centred?

All the activities in this book are learner centred. After considering how pronunciation will be introduced (see Tip 7 above), consider how to move the activity into the students' hands. How can they practise with each other? How can you move from whole-class drilling to an activity where students are producing the target language in smaller groups or pairs, or individually?

9. The level of the learners

The learners' level will affect the way in which you focus on certain features rather than what to focus on. For example, a consonant at the end of a word connecting to a vowel sound at the beginning of the next word (see **catenation** in Unit 21, pages 65–66) can be introduced at lower levels through combinations like *an apple* or *an umbrella* and at higher levels through phrasal verbs such as *look up* or *bring out*. In other words, consider the language you are using to introduce a pronunciation feature at a certain level, rather than deciding which features to focus on at which level.

10. How will students review what they have learned?

As with homework in general, we want to give students as much opportunity as possible to consolidate and review what we have done in class. This means considering how we can assign homework related to pronunciation and how useful that homework will be for them. This can be done through awareness-raising tasks, such as listening to a recorded dictation which contains specific features of pronunciation, or tasks where students record the target language and listen to themselves, or let the teacher listen to them and provide feedback.

Unit 3

10 ways to identify your students' pronunciation needs

When you know and understand your students' needs, your aims can be much more focused. This unit looks at ways of finding out what your students' pronunciation needs are.

1. Record and analyse

Perhaps the easiest way to find out about your students' pronunciation needs is to record them speaking and analyse the recordings. This means that you can listen to them more than once, and analyse their speaking and pronunciation in more depth than if you were just listening to them in the classroom. It also means that students can listen to the recording while looking at the teacher's feedback. Furthermore, it can be saved to show students how their pronunciation has improved over the duration of a course.

2. Ask them what they think the need

Students often know what they struggle with or what they are uncertain of so you can ask them to tell you about their pronunciation needs. They won't necessarily describe their needs using specialised terminology, but they might say something like, 'I find it hard to understand my work colleagues in the UK on the phone.' In this case, you learn that they have to communicate with UK speakers by phone, and then you can reflect that need in your lesson planning.

3. Ask them which accents they find hard to understand

It is much easier to ask students which accents they find hard to understand than to try to work it out based on listening tasks in the classroom. There are certain aspects of pronunciation that are fairly unique to certain groups of people, regardless of whether they speak English as a **first language (L1)** or not. Being aware of which accents students struggle with allows the teacher to include models of that accent in their lessons and to focus on the accent, rather than avoid it and hope that the students never have to interact with a person with that specific accent.

4. Find out which varieties of English they communicate with at work

Students often have to interact with speakers who use English as a first or second language as well as those you use different varieties of English. If there are specific accents that they frequently encounter in their work, it would be good to create an overall awareness of that accent, and look at why some people might find it difficult to understand. Your research could include finding out about terms that people from certain areas use; raising students' awareness of a particular variety can also help them to decode better when interacting with people from a specific geographical region.

5. Think about L1 interference issues

Consider what issues learners might have with pronunciation based on features from their L1. This helps with both positive and negative **L1 interference**. Some learners might find certain sounds or features of pronunciation easy if they exist in their L1; however, the more you know about the type of problems they are experiencing, the better you will be able to predict and diagnose problems before they arise, or at least to be aware of issues that could arise and pre-emptively address them through focused activities.

6. Ask a colleague to listen to recordings of the students

It's easy to get used to how your learners sound. This is especially true if you teach students who share the same L1, leading you to potentially ignore issues that could affect intelligibility. To mitigate against this, ask a colleague to listen to a recording of your students speaking. Ideally, choose a colleague who doesn't have contact with your learner group as they are more likely to provide insights into pronunciation issues that you might be missing.

7. Let students listen to their own recordings

Allow students to record themselves and listen to their own recordings. Doing this will allow them to hear how they sound and identify any areas of pronunciation they want to work on. They might identify parts where they don't like the way they sound. While the things they pick up on might not be serious issues, they still form part of identifying learner needs and addressing them.

8. Ask them when they misunderstand their classmates

When students are communicating with each other, there could be misunderstandings. Such breakdowns in communication are often used as opportunities to teach students conversation repair strategies; however, they also highlight aspects of pronunciation that could be exploited. Communication breakdowns caused by pronunciation issues may result from the speaker mispronouncing a word or from the listener missing something because of their own pronunciation issues. In both cases, misunderstandings allow the teacher to identify issues with pronunciation and address these in class.

9. Keep track of mistakes in listening tasks and diagnose the issues

Listening tasks in class are a great way for teachers to diagnose pronunciation issues. To do this, look at the questions that learners got wrong and find out what was confusing in the script. Don't focus only on individual lexical items; remember also to look at chunks and detractors that learners fail to decode due to a lack of familiarity with phrases or because of issues with connected speech.

10. Include pronunciation in every lesson

If you include pronunciation in every lesson, you'll find that you can focus on it consistently. Doing this will also highlight emerging needs and issues that might have been masked by other more serious pronunciation problems. A systematic focus on pronunciation not only helps learners improve, but also keeps the teacher informed of pronunciation needs as they develop, perhaps because learners have improved, or because their needs have changed.

Unit 4

10 pairs of pronunciation-related terms

If you are fairly new to teaching pronunciation, there is likely to be some unfamiliar terminology that you come across in this book. Don't be put off by it, though; if you think about it, it is no different from getting to grips with the terminology required to talk about grammar or vocabulary. To get you started, this unit takes a look at some of the basic terminology used for talking about pronunciation. You will meet many of the words again in later units, where we will go into much greater practical detail.

1. What terms do you already know?

For one minute, write down all the terms you have heard or read which are connected with pronunciation. Afterwards, cross out all the terms you are secure about. Then look at the remaining terms. Some of them might be provided below or in later units of this book.

2. Pronunciation and phonology

Pronunciation refers to the way we say words. **Phonology** is concerned with the study of the sounds we use in different languages.

3. Letters and phonemes

English has 26 **letters** in its alphabet with five vowels and 21 consonants. In the field of pronunciation, English has 44 **phonemes**. These phonemes are separated into 24 **consonant** sounds (for example, ʃ as in the first letter of the word _she_) and 20 **vowel** sounds (for example, **i:** as in _she_). With consonant sounds, the mouth restricts the air flow in some way (for instance, using the lips or the tongue). With vowel sounds the mouth lets the air through. (See Units 18–20, pages 56–64.)

4. Segmental features and suprasegmental features

Pronunciation is sometimes divided into these two sets of features. **Segmental features** are isolated segments, such as the phonemes in a word. **Suprasegmental features** go beyond single phonemes; they involve areas such as word stress, sentences stress and intonation.

5. Monophthongs and diphthongs

These are two types of vowel phoneme. A **monophthong** is a vowel sound where the mouth does not change when producing them; for example, **i:** as in _tea_. A **diphthong** is also a vowel sound, but this time the mouth changes while it makes the sound, moving from one vowel sound to another; for example, ɪə as in _dear_. (See units 18–19, pages 56–61.)

6. Place and manner of articulation

To produce the different phonemes, we use the mouth in different ways. Each sound it produces has a different **place of articulation**, for example, the place where the upper teeth meet the lower lip. The **manner of articulation** is the way in which the mouth makes the sound. It may involve friction between the upper teeth and lower lip; for instance, **f** as in _four_. (See Units 18–19, pages 56–61.)

Unit 5

7. Word stress and syllables

Every word can be broken down into a number of **syllables**. When a word has more than one syllable, one of the syllables will be stressed more than the others, resulting in a change of pitch. This is what is known as its **word stress**. For example, the word *phone* (**fəʊn**) has one syllable, whereas the word *phonology* (**fəˈnɒl.ə.dʒɪ**) has four syllables. The second syllable of phonology is stressed: phoNOlogy. (See units 13–15, pages 44–50.)

8. Stress-timed and syllable-timed

English is a **stress-timed** language, which means that certain words are stressed more than others; the stressed words are generally those that carry the main meaning of the sentence. This characteristic of stressing only certain words in a sentence is not true of all languages. For example, Italian is a **syllable-timed** language, which means every syllable is given more or less an equal amount of stress. (See Units 16–17, pages 51–55.)

9. Connected speech and intonation

In everyday speech, we don't pronounce individual words separately; we connect them. This means that two or three words might run together so that they sound like one word. Gaining a familiarity with the features of connected speech is particularly important for students who are developing listening skills. **Intonation** refers to the way the pitch changes when you say a phrase or sentence. For example, the pitch might rise to indicate that you are asking a question or that you are suggesting that there is more information to follow. (See Units 21–22, pages 65–70.)

10. Standard English and English as a lingua franca

The term **Standard English** refers to the version of English you might provide as a model. It could be British English or American English, for example. In recent years, this view of English has been criticised because it doesn't reflect the fact that many students learn English to use with other speakers of English whose first language is not English. For these students, it is argued that we should teach English as a lingua franca which differs from traditional standards of English. For the teacher, the question is: *Which English pronunciation are we teaching?* (See Unit 49, pages 145–146.)

"Pronunciation is the Cinderella of English language teaching. She is a kind of outcast, overshadowed by her two – also beautiful – sisters Grammar and Vocabulary. But when she is admitted to the party everything changes. There is a wholeness, and language and learning come alive as the feeling of real, embodied self expression becomes part of the game."

Adrian Underhill, author of *Sound Foundations* (2003, Macmillan Education)

Section 2:
The basic toolkit

In this section we give an overview of some of the tools and resources that are available to teachers when preparing pronunciation lessons. Some of the tools are those which – quite literally – we carry with us. Our own voice, mouth, hands and whole body are the essential starting point for any pronunciation teacher.

After that, we can help ourselves to help our students by making use of classroom tools and resources such as a board, a computer screen and projector, and published and online materials. Whether you are teaching in a face-to-face classroom, an online environment or in a hybrid context, you will find that most of the toolkit provided here will work.

To find out more about technological tools and resources for teaching pronunciation online, see **Section 5: Online teaching**, pages 117–130.

10 tools and resources

There are a variety of tools and resources available to language teachers and learners when working on pronunciation. Here is an overview of the ten most commonly used. You will see many of them referred to again throughout this book.

1. Your own mouth

The most useful tool for any pronunciation lesson is the one that carry with you – your own mouth. Some teachers are concerned that their own pronunciation is not quite the right model to give their students, and they would rather use recordings. But your pronunciation is as valid as any, so make use of it!

2. Mouth diagram

Although your own mouth can show the use of lips (and teeth to some extent), you will need a diagram to show what is happening inside the mouth. Some teachers put a diagram of the key parts of the mouth like the one below on the wall next to their board and point at it when necessary (see Appendix 6.2, page 150 for a full-sized version). (Note that there are other types of mouth diagram which highlight even more parts of the mouth – see Appendix 9 on page 151 for instance – but we have selected those which we feel are necessary and relevant for students to become familiar with to start off with.)

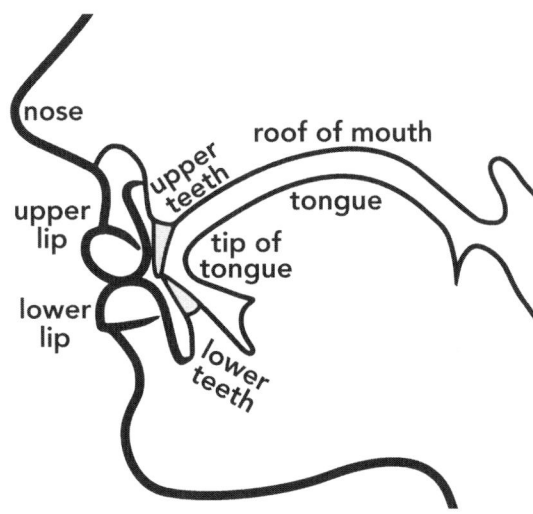

So, for instance, if you were teaching the sound **t**, you could point to the tip of the tongue and then point to the upper (or top) teeth to show where they are connecting to produce the sound. (See Unit 18, pages 56–58.)

3. Gesture

Fingers and hands can be very useful in a pronunciation lesson. You can count the number of syllables in a word on your fingers and emphasise the stressed syllable in a word by holding onto the finger that represents that syllable. Alternatively, you can count out the number of words in a phrase such as *I have gone home* on four fingers, and then squeeze fingers one and two together to show how the words *I* and *have* are contracted to produce *I've*. You can also use your hands to gesture the motion of the intonation pattern on a sentence by showing the rise and fall while saying the sentence.

4. Board work

When you write a new word or phrase on the board, you can place phonemic script over certain sounds, mark the word stress, or indicate the intonation. This kind of information is important for learners, but be very careful when adding it. Too much additional information on the board can cause confusion, so the key rule is consistency so that learners know when something refers to pronunciation. For example, it's often a good idea to use a different coloured pen or font for indicating word stress, or an intonation arrow so that learners don't think an additional mark here and there are part of the actual word.

5. Dictionary

The traditional printed dictionary will indicate the pronunciation of a word using phonemic script and marking the word stress with this symbol '.

crocodile (noun) C ˈkrɒkədaɪl
a large animal with hard skin that
lives in water in hot countries. It has
a long mouth and very sharp teeth.

Better still, a modern dictionary app on a phone will also play an audio recording of the word (often in a variety of accents). A good dictionary is an excellent self-study resource for a learner, so check what type of dictionary your learners are using and, if necessary, set aside some lesson time to make learners aware of how they can make full use of it for checking pronunciation.

6. Audio recording

Most learners can easily record their own voice on their phone. Having students record themselves and listen back can be a highly effective tool; see Unit 42 (pages 127–128) for more ideas on using recordings.

7. Video recordings

It's easy to make video recordings on a phone, too. Some teachers record their own mouths producing sounds and words so learners can watch and observe places of articulation. In addition, there are many similar video recordings on YouTube to help with this (see Unit 43, pages 129–130). Video recordings with subtitles can help learners when they are listening to everyday authentic speech, which may contain many features of connected speech.

8. Coursebooks

With so many of us working from coursebooks (both print based and digital), a lot of pronunciation work stems from exercises in the course materials. Many coursebooks incorporate a focus on this area with audio recordings and attention paid to the main aspects, such as sounds and word stress. Some online and digital versions also include functionality, such as recording yourself and comparing your intonation patterns with a model version. (See Unit 45, pages 133–136.)

9. Phonemic charts

Over the years there have been various versions of charts showing the 44 phonemic symbols and the way they relate to each other. One of the most influential is the chart created by Adrian Underhill in *Sound Foundations* (1994, Macmillan Education), which is divided into monophthongs, diphthongs and consonant sounds. Sometimes, you will also see charts showing phonemic symbols combined with an illustration of a word to remind learners what the sound is; for example, you might see the **i**: symbol drawn with the outline of a tree **tri**: around it. In trained hands, charts can be effective, but they are by no means universally used in classrooms.

10. The internet

Probably one of the most useful resources for teaching pronunciation is the internet. You'll find teachers producing phonemic sounds on their own YouTube channels, authentic recordings of TED talks (with scripts to allow you to read along), sites that play your favourite songs with gaps for you to fill in the missing words, and a huge range of tools to record your own or your students' voices. For many more ideas on exploiting this resource, see **Section 5: Online Teaching** (pages 117–130).

"I spend a lot of time creating resources for the pronunciation class, but I think maybe my favourite one was already there: it's the pronunciation the learners bring from their first language. Rather than being seen as something that needs to be 'overcome', the L1 sounds can be the foundation on which learners construct their English pronunciation."

Mark Hancock, author of the *PronPack* series (2022, Hancock McDonald ELT)

Unit 6

10 tips on using your voice

When it comes to teaching pronunciation, many teachers either rely on the coursebook with its recordings or they go online in search of 'model' versions of the pronunciation. But in fact, the starting point for pronunciation teaching is you and your voice. Here are ten ways to make effective use of it.

1. Use your voice as a model

You might be concerned that your 'accent' or way of speaking English doesn't match the type of English in the coursebook or the voices of speakers on the TV, radio or internet. But your voice is just as valid as anyone else's, so use it as the starting point. When you introduce a new word, say it for the students so they can hear how to say it.

2. The 'listen and repeat' voice

Initially, learners need to hear you say the word a few times, and then they need to repeat it. Teachers often worry that learners will get bored with this 'listen and repeat' approach, but at lower levels it's crucial and it can even be necessary at higher levels. This approach is also referred to as 'drilling'; we suggest ways to add variety to drilling in Unit 8, pages 31–33.

3. The silent voice

Sometimes it's useful not to speak aloud but instead to mouth a sound or a word without making the actual sound so that learners concentrate on the shape and movement of your mouth. You'll see this tip being used again in many other ways throughout this book, including for practising the shape of the mouth for different phonemes.

4. The robot voice

The robot voice is monotonous and has no intonation. When you want to highlight the importance of intonation in a phrase, for example, you can say the phrase once with a flat dull robotic voice and then say the phrase again, this time with intonation.

5. The humming voice

Another way to raise learners' awareness of what is happening in a phrase is to hum it rather than saying the words. That way, learners notice features such as sentence stress and intonation without being distracted by the content.

6. The contrasting voice

Saying a word in two different ways – in a correct way and in an incorrect way – is an effective method for drawing a learner's attention to what sounds correct. You can also use it to correct a learner. So, for example, you could pronounce the word *sofa* in two different ways to help learners stress the correct syllable, like this:

Teacher: Is it SOfa or soFA?
Student: SOfa
Teacher: Very good!

ETpedia: Pronunciation © Pavilion Publishing and Media Ltd and its licensors 2022.

Unit 7

7. The quiet and loud voice

Try to develop the ability to exaggerate certain aspects of pronunciation so they are clearly louder than other aspects. For example, if you want learners to notice where the sentence stress in the phrase *Can I help you?*, you can make the stressed word (*help*) much louder and the other words much quieter: *Can I HELP you?*

8. The attitudinal voice

For teaching intonation, it's helpful to release your 'inner actor'. When you say a phrase with different types of emotion or attitude, students really start to notice your intonation more clearly. For example, you might say the phrase *Can I help you?* in an angry voice, an excited voice, or with a caring voice.

9. Bringing in other voices

It is useful to bring other voices, so students are exposed to other accents and varieties of English. These voices might be recorded, but they could also come in the form of an invited guest to your classroom – perhaps another teacher, or someone who gives a talk on a subject. These other voices are an opportunity to share the richness of pronunciation with your students and help them to develop the skills they will eventually need to understand different English voices from all over the world.

10. The mimic voice

As you become more confident as a teacher, you will develop the ability to recognise the differences in the way someone speaks on a recording and mimic them. It's a helpful way to draw students' attention to such differences. For example, the word *hot* in British English is pronounced **hɒt** but in American English it has a longer vowel sound **hɑt**. Being able to isolate such features by mimicking them provides you with another useful addition to your toolkit.

"Faking your accent can be both unnatural and harmful. By using your own voice when teaching pronunciation, you encourage students to use theirs, which allows them to find their own identity."

Ku Yun Chang, teacher and young learners coordinator, British Council, Taiwan

10 ways to vary your pronunciation drills

Drilling in language teaching is often associated with boring listen and repeat activities where the teacher says a word or a sentence and the whole class repeats what they hear without having to think. However, drilling can be engaging for students and highly effective, for example, when it is used to draw attention to certain features of pronunciation such as a minimal pair or connected speech. The basic idea of a **drill** is that the teacher (or an audio recording) models the pronunciation and then students repeat what they hear. But that is only a starting point. Here are ten extracts of classroom drills to show the variety you can add. In each example drill, **T** = teacher, **S** = individual student, **Ss** = whole class.

1. Listen and repeat

The teacher drills the whole class, in this case with a single phoneme.

T:	ɑː		Ss:	ɑː
T:	ɑː		Ss:	ɑː

[T gestures to individual students and repeats the drill when S3 needs help]

S1:	ɑː
S2:	ɑː
S3:	æ
T:	ɑː
S3:	ɑː

2. Contrast drills

In this next example, the teacher contrasts a minimal pair in the drill.

T:	ɪ		Ss:	ɪ
T:	ɪ		Ss:	ɪ
T:	ɪ, iː		Ss:	ɪ, iː

3. Gesture drills

Adding gestures to a drill can also make a big difference. Here is the drill from Tip 2, but with the teacher adding simple hand gestures to contrast the short and long vowel:

[T holds palms close together to indicate a short vowel sound.]

T:	ɪ		Ss:	ɪ

[T holds palms wider apart to indicate a longer vowel sound.]

T:	iː		Ss:	iː

[T moves palms close together and then apart as they say each phoneme.]

T:	ɪ, iː		Ss:	ɪ, iː

[T repeats this drill a few times until eventually, they stop saying either phoneme but just moves their hands close and apart. As they do so, the students keep saying either ɪ or iː to match the position of the hands.]

4. Forward drilling

To draw attention to the features of connected speech in an expression like *Would you like a hand?*, it's often more effective to drill the phrase word by word so students build up the sentence, noticing features such as assimilation and linking as they go.

T:	Would
Ss:	Would
T:	Would you
Ss:	Would you
T:	Would you like
Ss:	Would you like
T:	Would you like a
Ss:	Would you like a
T:	Would you like a hand?
Ss:	Would you like a hand?

5. Backward drilling

For variety, repeat the process described in Tip 4 above, but build the sentence backwards:

T:	hand?
Ss:	hand?
T:	a hand?
Ss:	a hand?
T:	like a hand?
Ss:	like a hand?
T:	you like a hand?
Ss:	you like a hand?
T:	Would you like a hand?
Ss:	Would you like a hand?

6. Robot drilling

In this drill from an intonation lesson, the teacher has introduced students to the need for using intonation to express enthusiasm with certain vocabulary. So in the drill, they use a flat monotonous robot voice with no rise or fall but the students are expected to repeat it back to them with lots of enthusiastic intonation:

T:	[flat] That's amazing.
Ss:	[rise-fall] That's amazing!
T:	[flat] That's wonderful.
Ss:	[rise-fall] That's wonderful!
T:	[flat] That's incredible.
Ss:	[rise-fall] That's incredible!

7. Hum drilling

Humming the pronunciation in a drill can be very effective, especially with word stress, sentence stress and intonation. For example, a teacher could target the same language and intonation described in Tip 6, but this time the teacher hums the correct intonation without words, and the learners repeat it back adding in the words, like this:

T:	[rise-fall] mmm mMMMmmm
Ss:	[rise-fall] That's amazing!
T:	[rise-fall] mmm mMMMmmm
Ss:	[rise-fall] That's wonderful!
T:	[rise-fall] mmm mMMMmmm
Ss:	[rise-fall] That's incredible!

8. Mumble drill

When students learn to pronounce a word for the first time or try to say a phrase in a certain way, it's often useful to give them a few seconds to listen and repeat but not say it loudly. In other words, let all the students practise the pronunciation under their breath, almost like they are mumbling the word. This lets them focus on what their mouth is doing physically to produce the sounds without worrying about being heard by everyone else. With large, noisy classes, it can also be particularly welcome to have a quieter type of drill.

9. Error correction drill

If a student mispronounces a word or you think their pronunciation will affect their intelligibility, you can drill the sound, word or phrase on the spot with an individual student. Another approach is to repeat what the student is saying but with rising or questioning intonation, or with a missing phoneme. Notice both techniques being used by the teacher in this example drill. Instead of giving the student the answer, the teacher prompts the student by repeating the error and then providing the missing sound.

S:	I live in a 'ouse.
T:	'ouse? **h, h**
S:	house. I live in a house.

10. Online drilling

Pronunciation drills can also work with online lessons, but sometimes it's challenging when students experience a time lag caused by an unreliable internet connection. One benefit of live online lessons is that you can easily make recordings. If it isn't practical to do live drills of new words, end the lesson by reviewing all the new vocabulary and record yourself saying each of the words. Leave a one-second gap between each word, then share the recording file with your students. For homework, they can listen to you saying the words and repeat them in the gap you provided in the recording.

Unit 8

10 articulators of speech

One of the most useful tools you can have available for helping students to produce vowel and consonant sounds is a mouth diagram to show the different articulators of speech in detail. It's especially helpful when explaining to students what is happening inside the mouth behind the lips. It can also be a useful tool to help correct a student's pronunciation of a sound because you can point to the part of the mouth they are (erroneously) using and then to the part they should be using. Some teachers introduce the articulators of speech diagram on day one of a course and others introduce each part when it becomes necessary.

 Whatever your approach, you will need to introduce the ten parts listed in this diagram. You will find a photocopiable diagram to use and share with your students in Appendix 9 on page 151. (Note that there are other types of articulators of speech diagram which highlight even more parts of the mouth, but we have selected those which we feel are most necessary and relevant for students to become familiar with.)

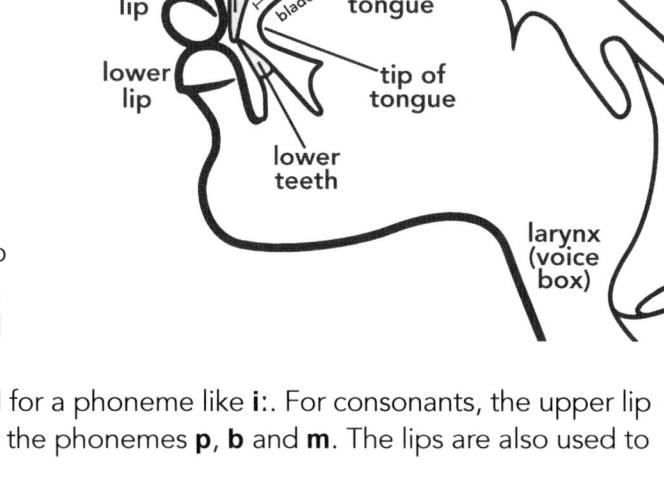

1. Lips

For vowel sounds, we use the upper lip with the lower lip in different positions. Sometimes they are wide and rounded to produce a sound like **ae**, and sometimes they are narrow and spread for a phoneme like **i:**. For consonants, the upper lip closes against the lower lip to produce the phonemes **p**, **b** and **m**. The lips are also used to make the semi-vowel sound **w**.

2. Teeth

The lower lip is used with the upper teeth for the consonant phonemes **f** and **v**.

3. Tongue

The tongue is used in many ways to produce sounds and so you will need to refer to different parts of it to help students. When teaching vowel sounds, you can talk about moving it forward in the mouth to produce vowels such as **ɪ** or **e**. Then you can describe moving it back slightly to the middle for sounds like **ɜ:** or **ʌ**. And finally, you can describe moving it back for a sound like **u:** or **ɑ:**. When it comes consonant sounds, you can go into more detail about the tongue by referring to the tip, the blade, the centre and the back. (Some books also refer to the 'front' between the 'blade' and 'centre' but for teaching purposes the four terms are enough.)

4. Tip of the tongue

To produce **θ** and **ð**, the upper and lower teeth rest together, and the tip of the tongue rests between the teeth and slightly closer to the upper teeth.

Unit 9

5. Blade of the tongue

Slightly behind the tip of the tongue is the blade of the tongue. When it rests against the alveolar ridge, you can produce **t, d, s, z, n** and **l**.

6. Alveolar ridge

By moving the tongue the blade just behind the alveolar ridge and towards the hard palate, you can then produce **tʃ** and **dʒ**.

7. Hard palate

The centre of the tongue rises up to touch the hard palate and produce the **j** phoneme.

8. Soft palate (velum)

Further back in the mouth, the back of the tongue pushes against the soft palate (also known as the velum) for the sounds **k, g, ŋ** and **w**.

9. Nasal cavity

For the sounds **m, n,** and **ŋ**, air moves through the nasal cavity because other speech organs are blocking it from moving out of the mouth. When learners produce these sounds properly, they'll be able to feel the cavity vibrating.

10. Larynx (voice box)

Further down into the neck is the larynx. Most people call it the 'voice box', and if you decide to refer to it with your students, 'voice box' is probably the better term to use. The vocal cords in the voice box can open and close. When they are open, they don't vibrate; this position produces the unvoiced (or 'voiceless') consonant sounds such as **p, f, t** and s. When the chords close (or are closer together), they vibrate and so we have voiced consonants like **b, v, d, z**. If students hold their fingers across the front of their neck when trying to produce unvoiced or voiced sounds, they become aware of the vibration, and in this way, they can judge how well they are making the sounds. We also use the voice box and the vocal cords to produce the friction necessary for the sound **h**.

"Learning about pronunciation and how sounds are formed is like the beginnings of assembling a jigsaw puzzle. Once you have all the pieces in front of you, you can see how they fit together, influence decisions and help recognition. Put simply, it's not just about how you say words, it's also how you recognise what people are saying to you."

Kirsten Holt, head of Pavilion ELT at Pavilion Publishing, UK

Unit 9

10 questions about mouth positions

The invention of the phone with a camera has revolutionised pronunciation teaching. It's so easy to take a photo of your mouth and share it with students so that they learn to recognise the shape of the mouth when producing an individual sound. You can also make short videos of your mouth with the recorded sounds. Alternatively, if you are teaching online, you can put your mouth close to the webcam and model a sound.

Here are nine mouth position questions with an accompanying question or instruction. The tenth suggestion is for the students to create their own. You can either reuse these images as they are shown here (see the photocopiable version, in Appendix 10, page 152) or create your own.

1. What letter is this person spelling?

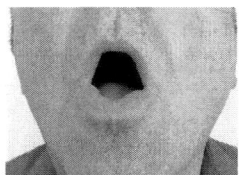

(Answer: The letter O.)

2. Which is the ɪ sound? Which is the ɑː sound?

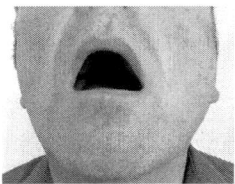

A.   B.

(Answer: A is **ɑː**, B is **ɪ**.)

3. Copy the action in the photo and say the phonemes f and v. What do you notice?

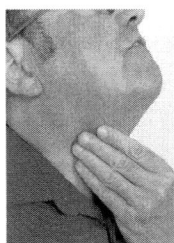

(Answer: The voice box vibrates with **v** but not with **f**. See Unit 18, pages 56–58 for more information.)

4. How does the person the photo feel? Ask the question: *Where are you going?* with the same attitude.

(Answer: The person probably feels unhappy about something. This activity is related to attitudinal intonation and the idea that our feelings affect intonation. See Units 23–24, pages 71–76.)

5. Is this person saying a consonant sound or a vowel sound?

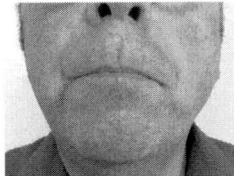

(Answer: To produce a consonant sound, the mouth blocks the air flow in some way; in this case the lips come together to produce a **b** phoneme. With vowel sounds, the mouth is open and so the air flows through. See Unit 18, pages 56–58.)

6. Notice the position of the tongue on the upper teeth.

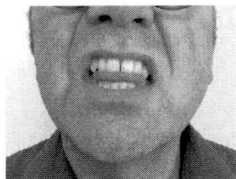

(Answer: Taking a photo lets you get very close so it's helpful with sounds such as **θ**, which are harder to demonstrate in a big classroom. See Unit 18, pages 56–58.)

7. What two sounds could this person be making?

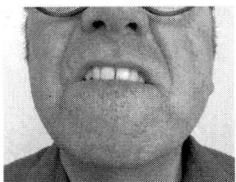

(Answer: The upper teeth are resting on the lower lip to produce the **f** or **v** phonemes. See Unit 18, pages 56–58.)

8. Put your hand in front of your mouth, as in the photo. Say the phonemes b and p. What do you notice?

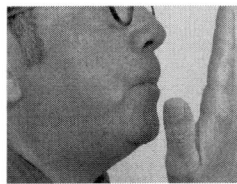

(Answer: You feel air hit your hand when you say **p** but not with **b**. See Unit 18, pages 56–58.)

9. Match the following words to the mouth positions A–C: *eat*, *are*, *not*.

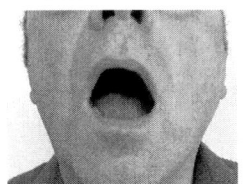 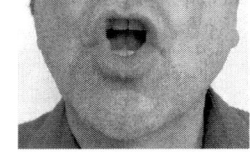 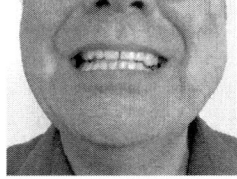

A.　　　　　　**B.**　　　　　　**C.**

(Answer: A. *are*; B. *not*; C. *eat*.)

10. Asking learners to create their own models

Having introduced the idea of taking mouth photos, ask your students to take photos of their own mouths while practising a set of sounds provided by you. Afterwards, they can compare their mouth photos with yours and decide if the shape is the same.

Unit 10

10 uses of the whole body

As well as using the mouth (see Unit 10, pages 36–37), a teacher can make use of their entire body for teaching pronunciation.

1. Count your fingers

Count out the number of syllables in a word or the number of words in a phrase on your fingers so students can both hear and see the number. The hand position in the photo might be used to show the syllables in a word like *banana* or a phrase like *Are you French?*

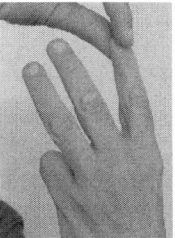

2. Hold a finger

Using the same technique as in Tip 1, hold on to the finger that represents a stressed syllable or a stressed word, such as *baNAna* or *Are you FRENCH?*

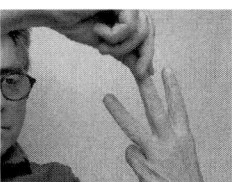

3. Hold fingers together

You can hold two fingers together to show where words are contracted or linked in a phrase. The hand in the photo shows how the words *I* and *am* are contracted in the sentence *I'm from Spain.*

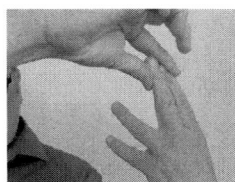

4. Hold hands close and apart

You can put your hands close together to represent a short vowel sound like ɪ (photo A) and then hold your hands further apart to indicate a longer vowel sounds like i: (photo B).

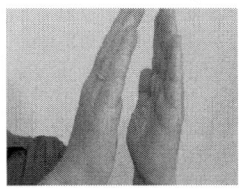 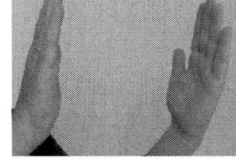

A.   B.

5. Punch the air

Punching the air can be used to show where the stress is in a word or a sentence.

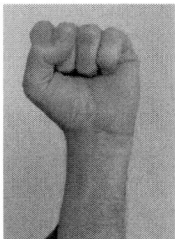

6. Clap

Clapping your hands can be used to clap out the stress in a word or the rhythm of a sentence.

7. Conduct with your arm

To show the rise and fall of the intonation in a sentence, you can move your arms along as you say the sentence (photo A) and raise it when the intonation rises (photo B) and lower it when it falls.

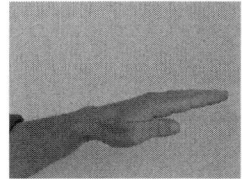 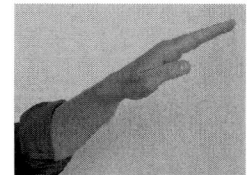

A.   B.

8. Sit and stand

You and your students can be sitting when they say a word or a phrase but stand up on the stressed syllable, stressed word or the rise and fall of the intonation.

9. Student line-up

If you are making students aware of the stress in different sentences, line them up so that each student represents one word in the sentence. You say the sentence and the students who think they represent a stressed word step forward when they hear it.

10. Make movements to make sounds memorable

When teaching the phonemes, it's often helpful to teach a movement to go with it. For example, in this photo, the teacher is introducing the **s** phoneme, so they make a movement with their arm like the movement of a snake's head as they make the sound. Other movements or gestures might include tugging on your ear when you teach the sound **ɪə(r)** or saying the sound **eə(r)** when you breathe out 'air'. Students can do the movements with you and they also start to make visual associations with the sounds. So, if a student is having problems with a word like *fear* or *clear*, you tug on your ear to help them remember.

ETpedia: Pronunciation © Pavilion Publishing and Media Ltd and its licensors 2022.

Unit 11

10 tips on using your board or screen

For most teachers, the board at the front of the class or the screen in the online lesson is a key teaching tool. Here are ten tips for optimising board work teaching pronunciation.

1. Plan the layout

The layout of your board work is crucial when it comes to teaching pronunciation. It can be a real challenge to both put up the written language you want to introduce and to add information about pronunciation as well; before you know it, the board can become cluttered and confusing.

2. Plan your board work

When you plan a lesson, try sketching out what the board will look like at each stage. That way you can see how much you will need to write on it and what the key pronunciation points you will want to add are.

3. Less is often more

Try to put the minimum amount of information possible on the board, and focus on one area of pronunciation.

4. Divide your board into sections

Some teachers draw a line down one side of the board to create a separate section for any incidental vocabulary that comes up during the lesson. As you add words into this part, you can mark the stress or add a schwa over a syllable in the word. By separating the board in this way, you avoid this extra information getting in the way of your overall planning.

5. Use colour

There is a danger that students might confuse elements such as written letters or punctuation with pronunciation symbols. One way to avoid this problem is to use different colours and to be consistent; in other words, you might always write your phonemic script in green, while the words are always written in black.

6. Be consistent

The previous tip stressed the importance of consistency with colours. Equally, try to be consistent with your way of presenting. For example, when teaching word stress, decide whether you are going to underline the stressed syllable of a word or write the letters of the stressed syllable in capital letters. Alternatively, you might want to draw little bubbles or dots over the stressed syllables. Whichever approach you choose, use it consistently from lesson to lesson so students don't get confused.

7. Be clear about what students need to copy down

Students are often unsure what they should copy down from a board. So be clear about whether you expect students to write a word down and whether they should add the word stress markers or the intonation patterns.

8. Be legible

When writing by hand on the board, make sure you are confident about writing in phonemic script, if necessary. With electronic whiteboards or screens, you might be typing. If so, you will find it useful to have a font for typing phonemes. You can download fonts for keyboards that will do this. Using the search term 'Type phonemes' will provide you with a selection of free online tools.

9. Ask 'Can you see?'

Be aware of where students are sitting and whether they can see the board clearly. If you start using different colours to add information about pronunciation, try to find out if any of your students are colour blind or have visual impairments. If necessary, offer them a seat closer to the board or change the colours you are using accordingly.

10. Reflecting on your board work

You can learn a lot about using the board for pronunciation teaching by looking at a teacher's board work at the end of a lesson. If you are able to observe another teacher, consider these questions as you observe:

▶ How much of the board work is dedicated to pronunciation?

▶ What did you like about the board work? For example, the clarity?

▶ What would you change about the board work?

As well as observing other teachers, try taking a photo of your own board at the end of a lesson or at different stages of a lesson. Then, a day or two later, have a look at the photo and ask yourself the questions above.

"When teaching Business English clients, students often have problems with the pronunciation of vocabulary that they have encountered in meetings, or new buzz words they're unfamiliar with.
So when they have a new word, I write it on the board (or screen), discuss the word, and help them to pronounce the new vocabulary including the British and American variations if applicable."

Evelyn Kreusch, teacher, Germany

Section 3: Knowledge and problem solving

This section provides you with key background knowledge to different aspects of pronunciation including information and ideas relating to word stress, sentence stress, individual sounds (or phonemes), connected speech and intonation. In addition, you will find a range of practical activities for introducing and practising these features of pronunciation.

There are tips on how to present aspects of pronunciation for the first time and how to predict what your students might find challenging. The activities described are often physical and fun, and, as such, they will form a memorable and effective part of your students' pronunciation journey.

10 things to know about word stress

This unit introduces you to the key aspects of what word stress is. Note that in some cases the tips will be tendencies and guidelines rather than 'rules' about word stress; as with many things in the English language (not just pronunciation) there are always a few exceptions to the rule.

1. What is word stress?

The term **word stress** suggests that the whole word is stressed. In fact, the term refers to the syllable in a word which is stressed. In the case of a one-syllable word, the whole word is stressed, but if a word contains more than one syllable, only one of those syllables is stressed. For example, in the word *banana*, the second syllable is stressed: *baNAna*.

2. Longer, louder, higher

When you the word *baNAna*, notice how the stressed syllable is longer and louder, has a higher **pitch**, and is pronounced with more clarity.

3. Primary and secondary stress

Some words have primary and secondary stress. **Primary stress** is the syllable that is stressed and **secondary stress** is the syllable that is less stressed, but not completely unstressed. For example, consider the word *delegate*: in the verb, **'delə͵geɪt**, the final syllable has secondary stress, but in the noun, **'deləgət**, the final syllable is unstressed.

4. One-syllable words

One-syllable words are stressed as a single syllable. This syllable usually retains the stress even if suffixes and prefixes are added to it; for instance, *WORK – WORker – reWORK – WORking*.

5. Stress on the first syllable

Some categories of two- and three-syllable words are usually stressed on the first syllable:

Two-syllable nouns: *TAble, ARMchair*

Words ending in *-ly* (especially adverbs): *LOvingly, NORmally*

Words ending in *-er*: *GARDener, MAnager*

Two-syllable adjectives: *HAppy, FRIENDly*

6. Stress on the second syllable

These categories of two- and three-syllable words are usually stressed on the second syllable:

Two-syllable prepositions: *beTWEEN, beHIND, beFORE*

Adjectives with a negative prefix: *unHAppy, imMOral, ilLEgal*

Two-syllable verbs are often stressed this way: *deNY, beGIN, proDUCE*

7. Stress on third-to-last syllable

Some word endings require the stress to come on the third-to-last syllable:

Words ending in *-cy*: *eMERgency; deMOcracy*

Words ending in *-ty*: *aBIlity, dependaBIlity*

Words ending in *-phy*: *phoTOgraphy, biOgraphy*

Words ending in *-gy*: *biOlogy, psyCHOlogy*

8. Stress in compound words

Compound nouns are usually stressed on the first syllable: *POST office, GREENhouse*

Compound adjectives are stressed on the stressed syllable of the second word, and often hyphenated: *old-FAshioned, bad-TEMpered*.

9. Word endings

Word stress falls on the syllable just before these word endings.

Words ending in *-able*: *WORKable, LAUGHable*

Words ending in *-cial*: *SOcial, fiNANcial*

Words ending in *-ery*: *BAkery, COOKery*

Words ending in *-ia*: *deMENtia, MEdia*

Words ending in *-ian*: *techNIcian, liberTArian*

Words ending in *-ible*: *CREdible, TErrible*

Words ending in *-ic*: *iCOnic, characteRIStic*

Words ending in *-ient*: *SAlient, inGREdient*

Words ending in *-ious*: *mysTErious, reLIgious*

Words ending in *-ish*: *SELfish, ENGlish*

Words ending in *-sis* (most often *-osis*): *osMOsis, hypNOsis*

Words ending in *-tial*: *diffeRENtial, prenuptial*

10. Stress on the final syllable

Notice how these word endings are stressed:

Words ending in *-ade*: *lemonADE, arCADE*

Words ending in *-ee*: *aGREE, guaranTEE*

Words ending in *-ese*: *JapanESE, TaiwanESE*

Words ending in *-eer*: *volunTEER, pioNEER*

Words ending in *-ique*: *uNIQUE, phySIQUE*

Words ending in *-ette*: *caSETTE, bruNETTE*

Words ending in *-oon*: *carTOON, afterNOON*

> *"Get your class to aim high in terms of pronunciation. Start by working on stress as learners report back with a sentence like, 'Her name is Sara, and his name is Marco'. Then, help them notice the music of the language and mimic phrases in a dramatic way, such as: 'Oh no! I'm so sorry! I've forgotten your name!'. Good pronunciation comes from good habits."*

Robert McLarty, teacher and editor of *Modern English Teacher* (Pavilion Publishing and Media)

Unit 13

10 tips for presenting word stress

When you introduce the idea of word stress in class, being consistent is the key tip. Be consistent in the way you present it and integrate word stress consistently into your lessons, rather than teaching it once and then not looking at it again.

1. Mark the stress

Here are some different ways of marking stress:

● ●● ●

com'puter   comPUTer   computer   computer   com / pu / ter   comPUter

There is no right or wrong way, as long as you are consistent, and your students get used to the way you show it. If you work with other teachers, it's a good idea to agree on a method so that students are not confused when they have a different teacher. If you are using published materials, it's a good idea to use the same form of presentation as the book.

2. Listen and repeat

When you are teaching a new word, students want to understand its meaning and use it correctly in a sentence. But for many, listening to it and being able to say it themselves is their first priority. Say the word and have the class repeat it. If necessary, add extra stress to the stressed syllable so they notice the stress.

3. Using dictionaries

Part of learner training is knowing how to use a dictionary effectively. In a print-based dictionary, the symbol ˈ is inserted before the stressed syllable like this: **kəmˈpjutə(r)**. An online dictionary will also allow the student to listen to and repeat the word.

4. Ask about the word

When introducing a new word, ask students questions such as: *How many syllables are there?* and *Which syllable is stressed?* For example, if the word is *emergency*, the answer would be *There are four syllables and the second syllable is stressed.*

5. Similar stress

When students struggle with a new word, suggest another word that they already know which has a similar word stress. For instance, *banana* and *umbrella* are both three-syllable words with the second syllable stressed.

6. Notice common patterns

As students build their vocabulary, start to draw their attention to common word stress patterns (see Unit 13, pages 44–45), focusing explicitly on patterns in nouns, verbs and adjectives. For example, two-syllable nouns are usually stressed on the first syllable, meaning that *apple*, *cabbage*, *armchair*, and *table* all share the same stress pattern. With higher-level learners, you can start to point out tendencies; for example, if a word ends in *-ity*, the syllable before this word ending is likely to be stressed. Identifying this this allows students to recognise and practise the pronunciation of other words with the same ending such as *accessibility*, *responsibility*, *proximity*.

7. Word forms and families

When you are teaching different word forms and word families with a root word like *photograph*, draw students' attention to the way the word stress might change from one word to the next within the set. For example: *PHOtograph, phoTOgrapher, phoTOgraphy, photoGRAPHic.*

8. Make it physical

Associating physical movements with word stress is a useful and fun way to notice the stress. For instance, if you are introducing *apple*, miming the action of taking a bite as you say the first stressed syllable of the word is memorable. Similarly, saying the word *banana* could involve miming taking a bite of a banana when students say the second syllable. Note also the photo suggestion in Unit 11.5 (on page 39), where the teacher punches the air on the stressed syllable.

9. Testing word stress

In spelling tests or quizzes, the focus is often exclusively on spelling. You can incorporate a word stress element by asking students to underline the stressed syllable in the words during a spelling test. Students can gain extra marks for providing the correct word stress.

10. Developing learner autonomy

When students review vocabulary, either in class or at home, encourage them to develop the habit of not just writing down the words for review, but also including the word stress. They can copy the techniques you used in your lesson, such as underlining the stressed syllable or writing the stressed syllable in capital letters. Alternatively, they could add colour, as shown in this student's notebook, where green letters have been used to highlight word stress:

Unit 14

10 activities for practising word stress

In the previous unit, we focused on ways of introducing and presenting word stress for the first time. In this unit, the focus is on ways of integrating word stress and offering opportunities for further practice, learner exploration and fun. You will find ideas for activities that students can do on their own, in pairs or in groups. Some of the activities also involve games, memory and movement.

1. Grouping the words

Review a lexical set of words you have been teaching recently. Write them randomly around the board. For example, here is a set of words for jobs and professions that are often taught at elementary levels.

teacher   manager   doctor   scientist   engineer   journalist

Next, write the following word-stress bubbles on the board. Students group the words by stress pattern, like this.

● ●   *teacher, doctor*
● ● ●   *manager, scientist, journalist*
● ● ●   *engineer*

2. Spot the odd one out

Following on from Tip 1, you can also show words in groups so that two words have the same stress and one word is different. Students have to delete the odd one out.

1. *teacher*   *doctor*   *engineer*
2. *photographer*   *scientist*   *manager*

(Answers: engineer and photographer are the odd ones out in their respective sets.)

3. Tap it out

Write a word containing more than one syllable on the board. Then demonstrate how to 'tap it out' by tapping with your right hand on your left shoulder and with your left hand on the table. The tap on the table is for the stressed syllable. So, for example, if the word is *devastation*, you would tap as follows: shoulder – shoulder – table – shoulder. Students practise this. Next, write a variety of recently taught words on the board. Students can try tapping these words while they say them, either on their own (but quietly) or together as a class. When everyone understands the idea, tap a stress pattern and ask students to say the word or words from the board that have that stress pattern. Finally, put students into pairs. In their pairs, they take turns to tap the word stress and guess the words.

4. Snap

Use the photocopiable in Appendix 15.4 on page 153 or prepare your own set of 20 to 30 cards with different words on. Students play in pairs or small groups so you will need one set for every pair or group. They deal the cards equally between them. Then, in turn, they put a card from their hand face up on the table and say the word on the card. If the two words have the same word stress, the first student to say 'Snap' wins the cards. The game continues until there are no cards and the winner is the student with the most cards.

5. Pelmanism

This game is a variation on snap (Tip 4). Use the photocopiable in Appendix 15.5 on page 154 or prepare your own set of 20 to 30 cards with different words on. Put the students into pairs or groups, each with a set of cards. This time, they put all the cards face down on the table. One student starts by turning over two cards. If the words on the cards have the same stress pattern, that student takes the cards and has another go. If the word stress doesn't match, the student turns the cards face down again, and the next player has a go. After a while, students start to remember the location of certain words which will match. The game ends when all the cards have been taken and the winner has the most pairs.

6. Categories game

Using the categories game in Appendix 15.6 on page 155 (or you can create your own version with recently taught lexical sets), put students into pairs or small groups. Give each pair or group the cut-up sets of words and ask them to categorise them into four lexical sets; in this case, the four sets would be types of meat, vegetables, rooms or places, and things in the house). Next, explain that students can categorise them again but by word stress. Avoid giving them too much guidance and let them work out how to categorise them.

(Possible answers:
Single-syllable words: *fish, beef, pork, lamb, duck.*
Two-syllable words with stress on the first syllable: *chicken, onion, cabbage, spinach, bathroom, bedroom, kitchen, sofa, armchair, bookcase, cupboard.*
Three-syllable words with stress on the first syllable: *broccoli, dining room, living room, balcony.*
Three-syllable words with stress on the second syllable: *potato.*
Four-syllable words with stress on the first syllable: *cauliflower, television.*
Five-syllable word: *refrigerator.*)

7. Dominoes

To prepare a set of domino cards, you can use the ready-made photocopiable version in the Appendix 15.7 on page 156, or create a similar set to practise recently taught words using the dominoes blank template on page 157. Students play in pairs or small groups and receive a cut-up set. They divide the dominoes equally between them and decide who goes first. The first student places a domino on the table. When they place a domino, they have to say the word on the domino. The next player has to match a domino using a word with the same word stress. If they cannot play, they say 'Pass.' Each time they place a domino, they have to say the word. The winner is either the first student to get rid of all their dominoes or the player with the fewest dominoes at the end.

8. Word stress race

Put students into teams of two or more. The teacher chooses a word stress pattern and uses sounds to demonstrate the pattern. For example, a two-syllable word with stress on the first syllable could be 'BOOM-ba', and a three-syllable word with stress on the middle syllable could be 'ba-BOOM-ba'. Students then have 30 seconds to write down as many words as they can think of with that stress pattern. For example, 'BOOM-ba' could produce *apple, pizza, armchair, table, burger,* etc. And 'ba-BOOM-ba' could produce *banana, umbrella, determined,* etc. Teams get a point for each (correct) word they think of. Then the teacher gives the next prompt. The time you allow for each pattern can be adapted depending on the students' ability, but should be short enough to keep the activity upbeat, and long enough to ensure each team writes down at least one or two words.

Unit 15

9. Line up

Choose a set of words (maybe a lexical set you have been teaching) and look at the word with the most syllables. For example, if the word with the most syllables is watermelon (four syllables), make groups of five or six students. Smaller classes can work as a single group. In their groups, students sit on chairs in lines. The teacher says one of the words, and students respond based on the word stress, starting with the student at the front of the line. There are three actions: Sit – Stand – Turn away. They stay sitting for unstressed syllables. They stand for stressed syllables. They turn away if they are extra and unnecessary (in other words, if they aren't required because the word is too short).

Here are some examples of how students should respond for certain words (assuming there are five people in the group):

apple: stand – sit – turn away – turn away – turn away.

banana: sit – stand – sit – turn away – turn away.

watermelon: stand – sit – sit – sit – turn away.

determined: sit – stand – sit – turn away – turn away.

Start slowly with this game and then speed it up. Also, you can move the students around after every word so that it isn't always the same students who have to turn away.

10. Word-stress table

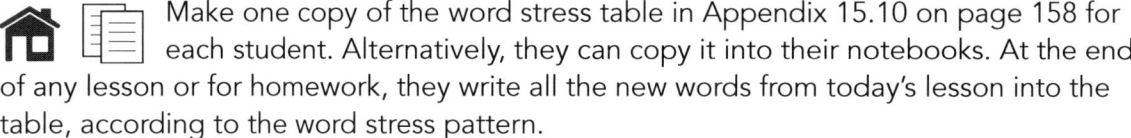 Make one copy of the word stress table in Appendix 15.10 on page 158 for each student. Alternatively, they can copy it into their notebooks. At the end of any lesson or for homework, they write all the new words from today's lesson into the table, according to the word stress pattern.

"You might notice that some of the students are having problems with the pronunciation of certain words. Write out the words you need to focus on, mark the stress on them, and then create a mini video where you go through the words. You can share the video with the students."

Russell Stannard, founder of teachertrainingvideos.com

Unit 15

10 things to know about sentence stress

This unit outlines the key points of sentence stress and explains why speakers stress certain parts of a sentence. It also highlights points to consider when first introducing this feature to your students.

1. English is a stress-timed language

In a stress-timed language, syllables are stressed (emphasised) at regular intervals. This leads to some syllables being much shorter than others, giving English a rhythmic a sound. If you want to demonstrate this to your class, ask everyone to clap the beat four times and say these phrases:

Dog, cat, fish, duck.

A dog, a cat, a fish, a duck.

A dog, and a cat, and a fish, and a duck.

A dog, and then a cat, and then a fish, and then a duck.

Make sure students are stressing the words *dog, cat, fish, duck* every time, and encourage them to notice that the time it takes to say the first set of words is roughly the same as the last set of words. That's because we increase the speed with which we produce the unstressed syllables in order to keep the rhythm the same.

2. Comparing English with syllable-timed languages

In contrast to stress-timed languages like English, other languages give each syllable in a sentence equal stress. These are called syllable-timed languages. You might find it helpful to draw students' attention to this so they can consider their first language (or other languages they know) and compare it to English. English and German are stress-timed languages, whereas Spanish, Italian, French and Cantonese are syllable-timed.

3. Content words are stressed

With English (and other stress-timed languages), the words that carry the main meaning – sometimes referred to as content words – are stressed in a sentence. For example, in the sentence *I went to the park by bus*, the content words are *went, park* and *bus*, and these words are stressed. When introducing the idea of sentence stress to your students, you can take isolated sentences from a listening, play them, and have students underline the stressed words. Then ask them what type of words tend to be stressed. These words are often verbs, adjectives and nouns.

4. Unstressed words

As well as asking students to notice which words are stressed, ask them to pay attention to the unstressed words. For example, in the sentence *I went to the park by bus*, the words *to, the,* and *by* are unstressed. Vowels in unstressed words are often produced with a schwa **ə** phoneme.

5. Secondary stress

The secondary stress is the word that doesn't carry the main stress in a sentence or chunk, but that is still stressed to some extent. For example, in the sentence *He bought a new laptop*, **lap**top carries the main stress, and *bought* carries the secondary stress.

ETpedia: Pronunciation © Pavilion Publishing and Media Ltd and its licensors 2022.

6. Emphatic stress

Having said that we often stress content words like verbs, adjectives and nouns, it's also important to be aware – and make your students aware – of the way we can vary the stress. For example, we can emphasise a certain word or phrase in a sentence to affect our meaning. A good example is the use of adverbs like *terribly*, *absolutely*, *extremely*, *completely* and *utterly*. Notice how the stressed syllable in a sentence like I'm EXHAUSTED. can change when you add an adverb and you want to emphasise the adverb, like this: I'm REALLY exhausted.

7. Shifting stress

We sometimes move (or **shift**) the main stress in a sentence in order draw attention to a different part of the sentence and its meaning. So, for example, you could emphasise the object of the sentence *I flew to PARIS*, or you could emphasise the verb, by saying: *I FLEW to Paris.*

8. Contrastive stress

Linked to the concept of shifting stress is contrastive stress. You use contrastive stress to highlight the difference between two ideas. For instance, stress pairs of words like it has been done in the following sentences to show contrast:

I flew to PARIS, not ROME.

Bob is my DOG, not my BROTHER!

9. The stressed syllable of the stressed word

When you are talking about sentence stress, it's easier (and more useful to students) to talk about which word is stressed in the sentence. In fact, it's the syllable of the stressed word, to be precise. In a sentence like *I flew to France*, this isn't a problem because *France* contains only one syllable. But in the sentence *I flew to Egypt*, the word *Egypt* contains two syllables, and it is only the first syllable that is stressed. However, when introducing sentence stress to your students, you might find it easier to refer generally to the 'word' that is stressed.

10. Stress on new information

When speakers are engaged in a conversation, they often stress the words that introduce new information. For instance, in the sentence *Sally bought flowers for Jane*, any of the words could be stressed to highlight new information related to the what the other speaker has said. Consider, for example, these questions and the way they are answered:

▶ Who bought the flowers for Jane? *SALLY bought the flowers for Jane.*

▶ What did Sally buy for Jane? *Sally bought the FLOWERS for Jane.*

▶ Who did Sally by the flowers for? *Sally bought the flowers for JANE.*

(Admittedly the answers above are unlikely, as most respondents would give single answers, but it demonstrates the stress we add to new information and raises awareness for your students.)

Unit 16

10 activities for practising sentence stress

The previous unit introduced the basic features of sentence stress and suggested ways to introduce it to students. This unit considers how you can expand awareness with further practice.

For more ideas on using chants and rhymes, see Unit 23 (pages 62–64) and Unit 25 (pages 67–68) of *ETpedia Young Learners* by Vanessa Reis Esteves (2016, Pavilion Publishing and Media).

1. Tapping or clapping

Tapping or clapping the rhythm of a sentence is a quick way to identify or draw attention to stress. You can take any sentence and identify the stressed words by tapping out or clapping a 4/4 rhythm. So even if a sentence has three stressed words, you can add an extra clap in the silence at the end, like this:

I had PIZZA for DINNER last NIGHT.   [silence]
        Clap   Clap   Clap   Clap

The rhythm can start slowly and increase, until students can produce the sentence easily at a normal speed. For fun, it can also be speeded up until it is really fast, especially with young learners.

2. Counting and underlining

During a lesson, isolate a sentence to focus on (for example from a listening) and write it on the board. Then ask students to listen again while you are reading it. Ask them to decide how many stressed words they hear and to underline them. It doesn't need to take up too much time, and should become a normal habit for students.

3. Contrastive stress dialogue

To introduce contrastive stress, write this dialogue on the board.

A: I'd like a chocolate and apple ice cream in a cone.

B: A chocolate and banana ice cream in a cone?

A: No, a chocolate and APPLE ice cream in a cone.

B: Oh, a banana and apple ice cream in a cone.

A: No, a CHOCOLATE and apple ice cream in a cone.

B: Oh, a chocolate and apple pie in a cone.

A: No, a chocolate and apple ICE CREAM in a cone.

B: Oh, a chocolate and apple ice cream in a cup.

A: No, a chocolate and apple ice cream in a CONE.

B: A chocolate and apple ice cream in a cone?

A: Yes.

B: We've sold out of cones. Sorry.

Discuss why the different words are stressed in each sentence. Then model the dialogue with a student, and let students practise the dialogue in pairs.

4. Build a dialogue

Following on from Tip 3, in which students have read and practised a dialogue, you could write a sentence (or selection of sentences) on the board with one stressed word, like this:

No, I went to Mexico for my JOB!

In pairs, students have to create a new dialogue which includes this sentence with its stress. Afterwards, they read out their new dialogues to each other and compare how they have used the sentence.

5. Teacher, you're wrong

Prepare three or four sentences that form a short story, or that are linked in some way, and write them on the board. For example:

Sally took a bus to the farm. She saw a chicken.

She bought some eggs. She used the eggs to bake a cake.

Now say each sentence one by one, but say a wrong word in every sentence. Invite students to correct you. For instance:

Teacher:	Mary took a bus to the farm.
Class:	No, SALLY took a bus to the farm.

Depending on the size of the class, students can either call out together or nominate a student. Continue like this:

Teacher:	Oh, that's right. Sally took a train to the farm.
Class:	No, Sally took a BUS to the farm.
Teacher:	Oh, right. Sally took a bus to the zoo.
Class:	No, Sally took a bus to the FARM.
Teacher:	Oh right. And she ate a chicken.
Class:	No, she SAW a chicken.

After this, put students in pairs and let them have a similar conversation.

6. Shifting stress meaning

This exercise shows how shifting the stress changes the meaning. Write the following questions and sentences on the board. Students match them correctly according to the stress. Encourage students to explain their answers. Then put them in pairs to practise asking and answering the questions and answers.

1. Would YOU like a blue and a red pen?
2. Would you like a blue AND a red pen?
3. Would you like a blue and a RED pen?
4. Would you like a blue and red PEN?

a. No, a blue and a red pencil.
b. No, not me, my friend.
c. No, a blue and a green pen.
d. No, just a blue pen.

(Answers: 1b, 2d, 3c, 4a.)

Unit 17

7. Add unstressed words

To draw attention to the way in which other words in sentences are unstressed, write groups of three words on the board, like this:

swimming – beach – Monday   *go – park – Tuesday*

practise – piano – Wednesday   *cook – family – Thursday*

tennis – friends – Friday   *baseball – TV – Saturday*

picnic – mountains – Sunday

Explain that these are stressed words from sentences. Students write sentences with these words by adding in words which will be unstressed. Then they practise saying them. For example:

We went SWIMMING on the BEACH on MONDAY.

Did you GO to the PARK last TUESDAY?

8. Text messages

Explain to students the idea that when we send text messages, we often write stressed words in capital letters. For example, here are three texts:

WHERE are you? My train is REALLY late. We've been waiting for AGES!

Put students in pairs and tell them to start a dialogue as if they are sending text messages (or if you allow phones in class, they could send real texts). The only rule is that they must capitalise one word in every message. (You might also want to point out that capitalising words in texts is sometimes impolite but it's OK between friends.)

9. Rhymes and limericks

Whether you're teaching young learners or adults, rhymes and limericks offer a fun way to draw attention to sentence stress. For example, young learners can chant a famous rhyme like this:

Hickory Dickory Dock.

The mouse ran up the clock.

The clock struck one,

The mouse ran down,

Hickory Dickory Dock.

10. Song lyrics

With higher-level learners, choose a song to use with your class and hand out the lyrics to students. (If the song is long, just use part of the song.) Working in pairs, students say the words out loud as if they were saying them normally and not singing them. They underline the (stressed) content words. Next, play the song. Students circle the words that are stressed in the song. Afterwards, the whole class discusses which words were only stressed because of the rhythm and the music, comparing the song's stress patterns with what they would expect in everyday speech. Ideally, choose an English song that you know your students are listening to a lot at the moment.

Unit 17

10 things to know about individual sounds

This unit introduces the basics of individual, single sounds (phonemes) with ideas on how to approach them with your learners.

1. What is a phoneme?

A phoneme is a single sound. When you put a series of phonemes together, you get a word. For example, the phonemes **p**, **e** and **t** said together produce the word *pet*. In this example, the symbols for these sounds look like the written spelling. However, other words, when written phonemically, do not. For example, the word *thought* written phonemically looks like this: **θɔ:t**.

Here's a complete list of the 44 phonemes in British English, with an example word after each (see Appendix 18.1 page 159 for a full-sized version). The part of the word in bold corresponds to the phoneme. The phonemes in the chart are split into vowel sounds and consonant sounds. The vowels are then split into two subgroups: **monophthongs** are vowel sounds where the tongue, lips and jaw have a single position. **Diphthongs** are also vowels, but the tongue (and sometimes the lips and jaw) moves during the production of the vowel.

Vowels (monophthongs)		Consonants	
i:	m**e**	p	**p**ut
ɪ	s**i**t	b	**b**ut
ʊ	g**oo**d	t	**t**oo
u:	y**ou**	d	**d**o
e	m**e**t	tʃ	**ch**ip
ə	**a**nd (unstressed as in *rock 'n' roll*)	dʒ	**j**ust
ɜ:	h**er**	k	**c**up
ɔ:	**or**	g	**g**et
æ	c**a**t	f	**f**oot
ʌ	b**u**t	v	**v**ase
ɑ:	c**ar**	θ	**th**ing
ɒ	h**o**t	ð	**th**is
Vowels (diphthongs)		s	**s**ip
ɪə	h**ere**	z	**z**ip
eɪ	**a**te	ʃ	**sh**e
ʊə	p**ure**	ʒ	vi**s**ion
ɔɪ	b**oy**	m	**m**y
əʊ	n**o**	n	**n**o
eə	**air**	ŋ	swimm**ing**
aɪ	**why**	h	**h**ow
aʊ	h**ouse**	l	**l**augh
		r	**r**ead
		w	**w**e
		j	**y**acht

First produced in *ETpedia*, pages 192–193 (2014, Pavilion Publishing and Media)

Unit 18

2. What phonemes do I begin with?

When you first start learning about or teaching phonemes, it can be rather overwhelming. After all, it's rather like learning or teaching a whole new language in addition to English. The main question many teachers ask is, 'Do I formally teach all 44 phonemes?' Rather than laboriously working your way through the whole set, a more effective approach you can take is to identify which phonemes your particular students might have difficulty with. In addition, consider whether any pronunciation issues they are having will affect their intelligibility. For example, if you have a student who tends to use the vowel sound **i:** instead of **ɪ**, the student might produce a sentence such as *The boxer heat his opponent* instead of *The boxer hit his opponent*. Although the student is choosing a longer vowel sound, it probably isn't affecting the listener's intelligibility because the context makes it clear what they mean. As such, you might decide not to work on that sound.

3. Integrate phoneme practice into lessons

Once you have decided which phonemes you want to focus on, try to integrate practice into your lesson planning, rather than making the whole lesson about one phoneme. You can quickly clarify the sound of a phoneme by showing the students a word they know well and pointing out the part that has that phoneme in. For example, when teaching **ŋ**, you can repeat words like *singing*, *dancing* and *running*, and exaggerate the *ing* part of the word. Another example is the **s** phoneme. Say words that clearly demonstrate its use, and exaggerate its position at the beginning of words such as *smoke*, *snake*, *school*, etc. (See **Section 4**, pages 77–115 on integrating pronunciation into lessons.)

4. Hold your vocal cords

To pronounce any vowel sound, the vocal cords will vibrate. In order for students to realise this, have them hold their vocal cords (around the region of the throat or larynx) between their thumb and index finger. Then get them to say some vowel sounds such as **i:** or **ɑ:** and they should feel the vibration. Next, ask them to pronounce two consonant phonemes such as **b** and **p**. They'll notice that the vocal cords vibrate with **b** but not with **p**. That's because **b** is 'voiced' but **p** is 'voiceless'. Students then try contrasting other pairs of consonants, such as **v** and **f**, or **z** and **s** while holding their vocal cords. They will notice the same voiced/voiceless difference. Being aware of the concept of voiced and voiceless consonants may help them if they struggle to produce or hear the difference between such pairs of sounds.

5. Feel the air

Different consonant phonemes require a different force of articulation. For example, the phoneme **f** is more forceful: it requires a strong rush of air forwards; the **v** sound, on the other hand, is soft, and does not. If students need help with more forceful phonemes, they can hold their palm near to their mouth to feel the stream of air that needs to come out. Another technique, which is messy but more fun, is to tear up a piece of paper into tiny pieces like confetti and hold the pieces in cupped hands. When you pronounce a sound like **p** or – even better – **h**, the strength of the air will blow the paper into the air.

6. Phonemes with something in common

Have students pronounce phonemes that have in common the parts of the mouth they use and how they are produced. For example, ask students to say **p**, **b** and **m**, in quick succession. Then ask them what the three phonemes have in common; in this case they all use both lips. If they say **ŋ**, **k** and **g** correctly, they are pushing the back of tongue against the soft palate at the back of the roof of the mouth.

7. Mouth the sounds

To focus the students' attention on the importance of the shape of the mouth in pronunciation – and in particular on the lips – tell them you are going to spell the name of a famous person but they won't hear the letters so they'll have to watch. Choose a person who will be well known to everyone in the class and spell the name using very exaggerated mouth movements so the spelling is very explicit. The activity is useful for demonstrating how the lips spread very wide on a letter of the alphabet like 'E' which is the **i:** phoneme, whereas the letter 'O' requires a rounded shape to produce the phoneme **əʊ**. Some letters are much harder to guess because they use phonemes that rely less on the shape of the mouth. This doesn't really matter; because you are spelling an entire name, the students can guess at some of the letters. At the end, ask them to say the name you were spelling. Next, ask students to think of someone famous. Working in pairs, they take turns to spell the names silently to each other, and practise using their mouth muscles.

8. Monophthong to diphthong

English has monophthong and diphthong vowel sounds, but some languages only have monophthongs or fewer diphthongs. To help your students hear the difference, choose a monophthong that also appears as part of a diphthong. For example, write **ɪ** and **ɪə** on the board. Point at **ɪ** and get the students to produce it. Then slide your finger over to **ɪə**. Continue to move the finger back and forth so the students repeat and contrast the changes in their mouth. They'll learn to feel how the tongue stays in the same position for a monophthong, but for a diphthong, it changes position.

9. Hold the jaw

As an extension to Tip 8, demonstrate that the position of the jaw also changes depending on whether a vowel sound is a monophthong or a diphthong. Ask the students to hold their jaws and contrast the position for the phoneme **ɪ** and **ɪə**. They should notice that the jaw needs to be lower for **ɪə**. They can try this out with other vowel sounds and discover the position of the jaw.

10. Miming and physical association

Try to develop a repertoire of mimed actions and anything that helps your students associate certain phonemes with movements. For example, if you need to encourage students to make a sound longer (for example, if they are saying **ɪ** but they should be saying **i:**, put your palms together and mime stretching them apart to indicate that the sound needs lengthening. Alternatively, the phoneme **z** resembles the sound of a bee so you could pronounce it while looking around your head for a bee. As you build up these types of associations, your students can be prompted to produce the sound from a gesture or mime that you use. There are no right or wrong associations, as long as you are consistent, and your students become familiar with them. Younger learners will also enjoy copying the actions.

10 activities for practising individual sounds

Following on from the previous unit, as students become more familiar with the individual sounds of English, you can start using these activities as a springboard for fun and engaging ways to help learners notice and practise individual sounds.

1. Quick quiz

As a warmer or five-minute filler in a lesson, put the class into teams. Say one vowel in isolation. Each team has one minute to write as many words as possible that contain that sound. Repeat the process for about five sounds (depending on how much time you have). Check answers at the end to find out which team wrote the most correct words. Note that answers might vary (and be correct) according to the pronunciation of words in different varieties of English.

2. Bingo

Design Bingo cards which use phonemes instead of numbers. Each student gets a bingo card that might look like this one, which practises the twelve vowel phonemes:

iː	ʊ	ɔː	ɜː
ʌ	ɪ	ə	e
æ	ɑː	uː	ɒ

(See Appendix 19.2 on pages 160–161 for the photocopiable version and blank template.)

The teacher reads out words randomly. Students tick a sound if they hear it in a word. When a student has ticked four phonemes in a row (vertically, horizontally or diagonally) they shout 'Bingo!' Repeat the activity a few times, and then put the students into groups. They play the game, with students taking turns to call out words with the sounds in.

3. What's the word?

Choose a set of words with the phonemes you want to focus on. For example, *sheep* for ʃ, *watch* for tʃ, *father* for ð, etc. Put the words on cards and put students in small groups of two to three students. Give each group a set of cards. The teacher says one of the sounds and students have to find the word that matches that sound and hold up their card. The fastest group gets a point. Continue until all the cards are finished.

4. Odd sound out

Give students lists of words which all have the same vowel sound, apart from one word which has a different vowel sound. Try to choose words with different spellings but the same sound. For example, the following exercise contrasts the phonemes əʊ and aʊ. The students either listen to or say a set of five words *though, snow, throw, house, hose* and identify the word that contains a different vowel sound from the others.

(Answer: house)

5. Identifying minimal pairs

Choose two sounds you want to focus on and write them at the top of the board. Then write five words containing the sound under each in a column, as shown in this example:

I	i:
bit	beat
flit	fleet
hit	heat
lip	leap
pit	Pete
sick	seek
ship	sheep
whip	weep

The teacher says words with either of the two sounds. Learners try to identify the sound. They can show their choice in any of three ways:

▶ They raise their left or right hand, depending on the side of the board the sound is marked on.

▶ They line up in front of the whiteboard and jump to the side of the sound. (This could be done with three sounds, where you have a sound on the left, a sound in the middle and a sound on right of the board.)

▶ They run or jump to the side of the classroom where the sound is (particularly good for young learners), and this could be done with a sound in each corner.

6. Phone numbers minimal pairs

Using the photocopiable in Appendix 19.6 on page 162, make one copy for each student. Model the task as follows: the students in the class say, *What's your phone number?* The teacher replies with the corresponding words. The students follow the words and write down the number. For instance, the teacher says, *lock, fish, sheep, chop, chop, shop, sheep* and the students write down 013 5563. Once students are sure of how the activity works, put them in pairs and let them do the activity together. Monitor for pronunciation and note down or correct pronunciation issues.

To focus on other minimal pairs, use the blank photocopiable on page 162. Prepare five sets of minimal pairs you want to focus on. Place each word on a number button on the handout.

7. Minimal pairs pelmanism

Students work in pairs or groups. Use the photocopiable on page 163 and cut up one copy for each pair or group. Students place the words face down. One player turns over two cards. If the cards contain words which are minimal pairs they keep the cards and have another turn. If not, they turn the cards face down again and the next player has a go. The game continues until all the minimal pairs have been matched.

8. Dice

Take pairs of dice and stick different phonemes on the six sides. You could put consonant phonemes on one die and vowels on the other. The students roll a pair of dice. They win a point if they can make a word which contains both phonemes. For example, if they rolled ʃ and **aɪ**, they could make the word *shine*.

9. Pronunciation selfies

Understanding how your mouth moves helps greatly in producing individual sounds. This also helps with vowel quality. Students can use their phones (as if they were taking a selfie) either in the classroom or at home. They record themselves and notice their mouth movements when producing sounds and words. They compare these with other examples available online in video format. The selfie video allows them to notice how their mouth is moving while they are producing certain sounds or words, helping them to become more aware of how they are producing certain sounds.

10. Recording words with the sounds

Give each student a copy of the phonics chart in Appendix 19.10 on page 165. In class, check they can say the individual sounds, and then the words with those sounds in.

For homework, they start to write other words that contain the individual sounds into the third column in the chart. They could also add new words to these lists as they come across new vocabulary during the course.

"When made aware of differences in how sounds are made, students start to differentiate the vowels that previously sounded the same to them. This is particularly important for my students because Japanese has a much smaller vowel inventory than that of English."

Peter Iori Kobayashi, associate professor, Department of International Studies, Niigata University of International and Information Studies, Japan

10 reasons why learners have problems with individual sounds

In the two previous units we looked at what phonemes are (individual sounds) and how we might present and practise them with our learners. It's also important to stress that different learners will have differing difficulties (and successes!) with different sounds. So sometimes you might not need to spend much time on sounds which aren't affecting **intelligibility** because your class is made up of learners with a first language which is similar to English in many ways. Alternatively, if you know where a student is from and their first language, you can often predict with some accuracy the challenges they may face. This unit introduces some of the reasons why learners might have problems with certain individual sounds. For a more detailed explanation of learner difficulties with pronunciation according to their first language, refer to the excellent book *Learner English* (referenced in Unit 50.3, page 147).

1. Sounds don't exist in the learners' L1

English has a significant number of phonemes (individual sounds) compared with many other languages. This means there is a likelihood that there are sounds in English that do not exist in learners' first languages (L1s) that may cause **L1 interference**. For example, there is a difference between the two initial sounds in the words *pat* and *bat* in English, but in some languages (such as Arabic), the distinction between **p** and **b** does not exist to the same extent it does in English so Arabic speakers may hear them as the same word.

2. Sounds exist in the L1 but are used differently

Sounds that appear in clusters or at different parts of a word (initial, mid or final) differ across languages. For example, the phonemes **b**, **p**, **d**, **t** and **l** all exist in Mandarin Chinese, but never appear in a mid or final position. While Mandarin Chinese speakers might have no problem pronouncing these sounds in initial positions, they might struggle with them in final positions and have a tendency to add a schwa sound to the end of these sounds, producing an additional syllable; for example, *cat* might become *ca-te*.

3. Similar sounds in L1 confuse learners

Some sounds do appear in a learner's L1 but they sound a bit different and are formed differently. For example, while there is a 'r' sound in Mandarin and Cantonese, it is **retroflex**, meaning the tongue is curled backwards at the start of the sound. When Chinese characters are transcribed into the Roman alphabet, the sound is written as 'r' but it is pronounced significantly differently from the **r** phoneme we produce in English. This written convention could confuse learners or mislead them into believing that the sounds are produced similarly, when in fact, they are not.

4. Sounds are not perceived in L1

Sounds might be perceived as similar within a language when they are actually different. For example, the **p** phoneme in *pot* is pronounced differently from the **p** phoneme in *spot* as the aspiration is not the same. While it makes little-to-no difference to speakers of English (as the difference in **aspiration** does not change meaning), there are languages where this change in aspiration could change the meaning of a word. Cantonese is one example of a language where aspiration of the **p** changes the meaning of a word.

5. Where and how the sound appears in a word

As discussed under Tip 2, the place where a letter appears could create problems for learners. This could simply be because it might be difficult to remember which sound to produce depending on where a sound appears. Consider, for example, the pronunciation of the letter 's' in *leisure*, play**s**, *immersion*, *walks*, and **s**now and how it varies when pronounced.

6. Stress-timed and syllable-timed

As English is a stress-timed language (see Unit 16.1, page 51), words and sentences always contain a number of weak forms or unstressed syllables. This might present a problem for learners. Learners with an L1 that is syllable-timed (in other words, where each syllable takes roughly the same amount of time to say) may find it difficult to identify the weak forms in speech, and have trouble producing them. For example, if a learner has learnt 'go to bed' as three stressed sounds, and then they hear the same phrase with the word *to* unstressed, they may struggle to piece together what was said.

7. The schwa and unstressed syllables

Following on from Tip 6, another problem is that the schwa sound (ə) is perceived as one sound in English, but it isn't always pronounced in exactly the same way. For example, while it makes no difference to speakers for whom English is their first language, L1 speakers of some languages will hear the subtle pitch and tone changes that occur between the first and last syllables of a word like 'banana'. This is because their language distinguishes between those two sounds. Note also that the unstressed vowel is not always a schwa sound. For example, in the word *roses* 'rəʊzɪz, the second syllable is unstressed but it doesn't contain a schwa sound.

8. Inversion of sounds in consonant clusters

A **consonant cluster** occurs when consonant letters are grouped together in a word with no vowels in between (See tip 10 on page 64 for consonant blends). Sometimes, a speaker will mistakenly invert the sounds in consonant clusters. For example, notice the difference between the clusters **ks** and **sk** in the words *tax* and *task* or *axe* and *ask*. While it is often easy to understand what is meant from context, this is not always the case: for example, there would be a significant difference in meaning if the manager were told to *ask him* or *axe him*. This can be a problem for learners if they have certain consonant clusters they are used to saying in their own language which are different from those in English. Typically, this might affect students with a Slavic language as their first language (L1).

9. Identifying sounds in speech

The way in which sounds are perceived and produced across different varieties of English can create problems for learners, especially in terms of identifying sounds or words. Consider, for example, the pronunciation of *water*, which differs across varieties of English: some varieties drop the **t** and fill it in with a glottal stop; others pronounce the 't' sound a bit like **d**.

Unit 20

10. Aspiration in consonant blends with 's'

Aspiration is when the act of saying a consonant sound involves pushing air out, such as in the sounds **t**, **p** or **k**. (Try saying them with your hand in front of your mouth and you'll feel the air.) However, when you blend these sounds with **s**, they lose their aspiration because the s sound is not aspirated. For instance, aspirated sounds that blend with *s*, such as **st**, **sp**, and **sk** lose their aspiration, and this means that **st** can sound similar to **sd**, **sp** can sound similar to **sb** and **sk** can sound similar to **sg**. Students who speak a first language that has both an aspirated and unaspirated **p**, **t**, or **g** sound might find it difficult to distinguish between the sounds, but even L1 speakers can mishear or misinterpret what it said. A famous example of this is in the lyrics to the Jimi Hendrix song 'Excuse me while I kiss the sky', which is sometimes heard as 'Excuse me while I kiss this guy.' The simple reason for this is that the aspiration of the **k** that follows the **s** makes it sound like **sg** because of the lack of aspiration. There are lots of other examples, for example hearing 'the lions bed up' instead of 'the lion sped up' or in answer to 'What's this?' the difference between 'It's stock' or 'It's dock.' Sometimes, students try to overcompensate, or they struggle with the blend and pronounce a word like *student* as ˈsətjuːdənt.

Note the term **constant blends:** The term **consonant cluster** refers to two or three consonants next to each other in a word. When we say 'cluster', we refer to the written form, and when we say 'blend' we refer to the spoken form. Many teachers use the term **consonant cluster** (not blend) to refer to both the written and spoken form.

"Based on my teaching experience of over 30 years, I'd say that many of my Turkish students have good grammar and good written English but pronunciation is more of a challenge. Their problems with English pronunciation is affected by several phonological features which lead to common errors when they speak. The most common are with diphthongs and adding extra vowel sounds."

Evrim Üstünlüoğlu, associate professor, Izmir University of Economics, Türkiye

10 key terms for describing and presenting connected speech

The next two units look at connected speech. This unit highlights some key terms that teachers can use to describe connected speech. It also suggests some activities for practising specific aspects of connected speech. Look at this photo of the whiteboard from a real lesson. Use the tips below to help you identify which features of connected speech the teacher has indicated to her students.

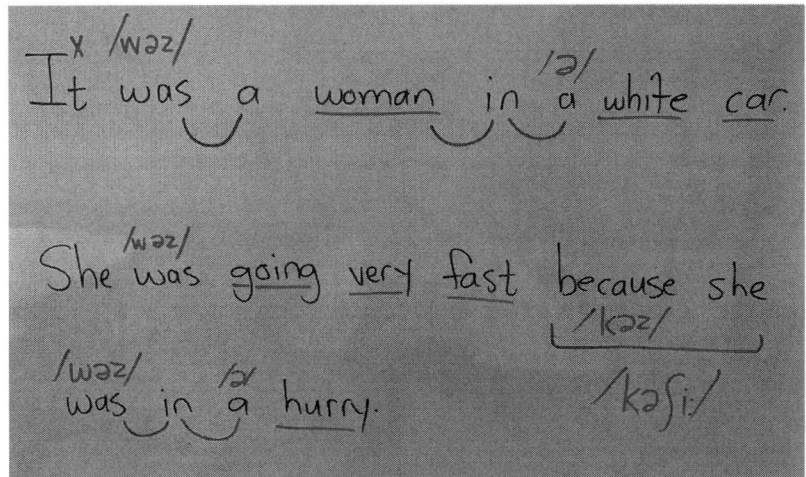

(Thanks to Sandy Millin for sharing the image from her class.)

Unit 21

1. Stress and unstress

Stress is a key component of connected speech. If you listen to a sentence like *It was a hot day*, you'll notice that the two words *hot* and *day* are stressed. The words *it was a*, on the other hand, are not stressed, to the point that we might barely hear them, and the vowel sounds in the words *was a* are likely to be unstressed.

2. The schwa

If we transcribe the sentence *It was a hot day* using phonemic script, it would probably look like this: **'ɪt wɒz ə 'hɒt 'deɪ**. But when we say the sentence, we might say it more like this: **'ɪt wəzə 'hɒt 'deɪ**. Notice how certain vowel sounds are being replaced with this symbol **ə**, called a **schwa**. It represents unstressed vowel sounds in an utterance.

3. Rhythm

As we can stress and unstress sounds in English (See Unit 16 on pages 51–52, in particular Tip 1: English is a stress-timed language) utterances have a **rhythm**; for example, if you count out three regular beats and repeat the sentence *It was a hot day* a few times, you'll notice that the words *It was a* take up one beat, *hot* another beat, and *day* the final beat.

4. Assimilation

One effect of stress and unstress is that one phoneme might change in order to accommodate the phoneme that follows. For example, if you hear the word *cupboard*, you don't hear the two syllables *cup* and *board* separated. Instead, most speakers will tend to change the sound of the *p* to accommodate the sound of the *b* that follows, to produce **kʌbəd**. This feature is referred to as **assimilation**.

5. Partial assimilation

Another form of assimilation is when the phoneme changes to another phoneme but a different phoneme from the one next to it. For example, at speed, *can play* will sound like *cam play*. The **n** changes to a **m** sound due to bilabial **p** that follows it. This is sometimes referred to as **partial assimilation** rather than the example of **complete assimilation** in Tip 4.

6. Elision

Elision is when a sound completely disappears. (We say the sound is 'elided'.) This often happens with identical sounds next to each other, for example, the first **t** in *next to*, which is pronounced **nekstu:** rather than **nekst tu:**. However, elision can also occur when two sounds next to each other are different; for example, the **d** in *stand by*, which is elided when the two words are said together.

7. Linking or catenation

Linking, also referred to as **catenation**, occurs when the last consonant sound of a word links to, and moves over to, the start of a word that begins with a vowel. For example, at speed, *an apple* would sound like **əˈnæpl**. This example of connected speech illustrates that even lower-level learners should be made aware of linking as it affects beginner-level language, such as the article *an* and a following word that starts with a vowel.

8. Intrusion

Intrusion occurs when a new sound is inserted between two words in order to connect them. For example, if you listen to a speaker say the phrase *I saw a movie*, you'll hear that the words *saw* and *a* are linked (see Tip 7). But in addition, you might not hear the *w* at the end of the word *saw*. Instead, you might hear a **r** sound. We can indicate this intrusive *r* sound to our students like this: 'I saw‿r‿a movie.'

Two other examples of intrusion involve inserting a j and a w sound. For example, we might add the **j** sound between *I* and *am* to produce 'I‿j‿am'. And your learners might hear the **w** sound between *go* and *up* in 'go‿w‿up'.

9. Linking r

As a follow-up to Tips 7 and 8, note that some words might end with the letter *r* (such as the word *four*), but in many accents of English you don't hear it when someone says the word in isolation. However, if someone says *four animals*, they do pronounce the *r* at the end of *four*, and it sounds like 'four‿r‿animals'. This feature is similar to intrusion, but because the word already has the letter *r* in it, it is referred to as **linking**.

10. Contractions

Probably the most common aspect of connected speech that teachers deal with on a daily basis are contractions. Contractions are very common in English and happen mostly with a pronoun and an auxiliary verb (for instance, *they are* –> *they're*) or an auxiliary verb and *not* (*is not* –> *isn't*). The feature is so common in English that is also a formalised part of written English, and it is indicated with an apostrophe.

Unit 21

10 ways to introduce and practise connected speech

Following on from Unit 21, this unit focuses on activities that practise connected speech. It's worth stressing that connected speech is a feature of the pronunciation of only some speakers of English. For example, people who use English as their first language (L1) will usually connect their speech. On the other hand, the many users of English as a second language, or those who have learned it later in life, will often separate out the words more. When teaching, your main focus should be on helping learners to listen to and understand connected speech rather than trying to get them to reproduce it. That said, attempting to reproduce connected speech can help to increase their awareness of the features.

1. Drilling

Even with beginners, it can be useful to highlight a feature of connected speech by quickly drilling two words which are connected. For example, if you introduce a mini-dialogue, where students are going to ask and answer *What's this?* and *It's a/an …*, drill the words with the article *a* or *an* so that students get used to hearing and possibly saying *It's‿an‿apple* rather than separating out every word like a robot, as in *It / is / an / apple*.

2. Contrast two versions

Following on from Tip 1, say the same sentence twice – first in a natural, connected, way, and then in a separated, 'robotic' way. For example:

[natural]:	It's‿an‿apple.
[separated]:	It / is / an / apple.

Then ask students which sounds better or more natural. Note that the second, 'separated', version is not incorrect; it's just a question of drawing a student's attention to what they are hearing.

3. Dictation

As an alternative or extension to the activity in Tip 1, say the phrase at normal speed and students write down what they hear so it becomes a dictation exercise.

4. How many words do you hear?

Choose a sentence from a recording or choose your own phrase (or utterance) which contains connected speech. Repeat the phrase a few times. Students count how many words they hear. You can count contracted forms as one word. For example, if you say the sentence *I'll see you at eight*, the students call out *Five words!* Alternatively, they could hold up the correct number of fingers or they write the number down.

Afterwards, you could write the phrase on the board to highlight that it contains a contracted form, an intrusive **w** and linking, like this: *I'll see you‿**w**‿at‿eight*.

5. Mark the stress and the schwa

As a follow-up to the work done in Tip 4, write the phrases you have said on the board. Then say them aloud again and ask students to underline the stressed words in the phrase and identify any weak forms with a schwa. For example:

ə

I'll <u>see</u> you at <u>eight</u>.

6. What is connecting?

As students start to become more familiar with the features of connected speech, you can drill sentences from the last word or chunk where connected speech happens. Then, as you go along, ask students what is connected and how the connected words sound different from the two separate words. Move backwards towards the start of the sentence stopping at every word or chunk where connected speech happens. For example, you might introduce the phrase *Meet me at the box office* like this, with students identifying the feature (shown in brackets) at each stage:

box‿office (linking between letters *x* and *o*)

at‿the box office (elision of the **t** in *at the*)

Meet me‿at the box office (intrusive **j** between *me* and *at*)

7. Mini dialogues

Write *You've got to tell her!* and *I don't know where it is.* on the board. Elicit and drill the pronunciation of the two sentences, focusing on connected speech. For example, *You've got to tell her!* is pronounced as **juːv ɡɒtəˈtɛlhɜː** and *I don't know where it is.* is pronounced as **aɪ dənəʊ weə rəˈtɪz**. Then, in pairs, students prepare a mini-dialogue where the sentence appears (even if it is the last sentence). Students practise their dialogues and present them to the class. Focus both on the pronunciation of the target phrases and also on the pronunciation of other sentences in their dialogues.

Example dialogues could be:

A: I accidentally broke my mum's special cup.

B: You've got to tell her. (**juːv ɡɒtə ˈtelhɜː**)

Or

A: Where's your book?

B: I don't have it.

A: But you need your book for class.

B: I know, but I don't know where it is. (**aɪ də'nəʊ weə rə'tɪz**.)

To adapt the activity, use sentences you have recently taught.

8. I can't hear you!

The purpose of this activity is to make students aware of how to disconnect their speech. This may appear counter-intuitive, but it actually helps to create a much better awareness of connected speech. Select a few phrases that students might use during a phone call, in a conversation in a nightclub, or while chatting at a football match. Drill the phrases, focusing on connected speech. Put students in pairs and model a quick role play, where you say one of the phrases and a student replies with *I can't hear you*. You then repeat the phrase more slowly without connected speech. Ensure students understand that you are doing this because you are in a noisy place or on the phone. You could play music in the classroom while they are working in pairs to add to the effect. An example exchange might be:

A: Do you want to watch a movie after the match?

B: I can't hear you.

A: [Slower and more clearly enunciated] Do you want to watch a movie after the match?

9. Phrasal verbs noughts and crosses

Linking or catenation is a common feature with phrasal verbs between the main verb and the following preposition or particle if it starts with a vowel sound, for example, *look‿up (something on the internet)*. You can play a version of noughts and crosses that draws students' attention to this. Draw the following grid on the board (or create your own version).

blow up	call off	find out
hold up	put away	make up
look up	set up	hand in

Put students into two groups (one group is 'crosses' and the other is 'noughts') and show them the nine phrasal verbs. The teams take turns to choose a phrasal verb and make a correct sentence with it. They also have to try and say the phrasal verb with linking; for instance, *Let's look‿up the word in a dictionary*. If you are happy with the sentence and the pronunciation, place a cross or a circle in the square and move to the other team.

To adapt the activity, select other multi-word verbs, or any phrases where connected speech happens; for example, binomial pairs like *black and white* or *salt and pepper*.

10. A listening gap-fill exercise

You can use a classic gap-fill exercise for drawing attention to connected speech. Either choose a short listening (perhaps one you have already used from the coursebook) or read out a text. If you choose to read a text, make sure you are consistent with your connected speech. Before the lesson, take the listening scripts and create a gap-fill version by removing any word that is linked to the one before. For example, compare this extract from a recorded audio script with the gapped version given to students:

Audio script

When we talk about high tide and low tide, we're referring to the rise and fall of the sea. High tide is when the sea covers the beach, rising to its highest level, and low tide is when it moves away, leaving the beach uncovered.

Gapped script

Listen and complete this text.

When we talk _____ high tide and low tide, we're referring to the rise _____ fall _____ the sea. High tide _____ when the sea covers the beach, rising to _____ highest level, and low tide _____ when _____ moves _____, leaving the beach _____.

Play the recording or read out the text. Students write the missing words in the gaps. Doing this draws their attention to the linking feature, and helps to develop their listening skills.

> *"Comparing the speech with the text is a great way of 'noticing'. Students can notice how words sound different when they are in connected speech and there's no 'white space' between them."*
>
> **Jane Ward, teacher, UK**

10 things to know and consider about intonation

Notice that the title of this unit refers to things to know; it's unlikely that you will formally teach your students many of the ten points listed here. In class, teaching intonation normally involves raising students' awareness that pitch in a phrase or sentence rises and falls. Sometimes a speaker might change the intonation of an utterance, and in doing so change its meaning. The ability to notice and understand these changes are part of a student's progression to more advanced levels of English.

1. The tone unit (or intonation group)

The **intonation group** or **tone unit** is a basic part or chunk of language; it might be a single word, a phrase, a whole sentence, or even just part of a sentence. Within it, there will be one complete movement of intonation. In the classroom, it's often helpful to identify intonation groups so that you can deal with individual intonation patterns rather than overwhelming students with long pieces of text and different intonation. All of these are examples of intonation groups (also sometimes referred to as tone units):

//Help!/

//Can you help me?//

//I was wondering if you could help me.//

2. The tonic syllable (or nucleus)

In a tone unit, one syllable will always have the most stress. This stressed syllable is where the intonation will be most prominent. This is called the **tonic syllable** of the intonation group (or the **nucleus of the tone unit**):

//Can you help me?//

3. The head (or onset syllable)

The head of an intonation group is the second most prominent syllable in the intonation group (in the utterance below, it's *Can*). This is where the pitch starts rising; it rises all the way to the nucleus (*help*). This pitch is sometimes referred to as the **key**.

//Can you help me?//

4. The pre-head and tail

The **pre-head** refers to any syllables that come before the head; **the tail** refers to those that come after the nucleus. So in the example below, *I was* is the pre-head, *wondering* is the head, *help* is the nucleus, and *me* is the tail.

//I was wondering if you could help me?//

5. Intonation patterns

For the purposes of teaching, we talk about the four main intonation patterns of English: rise, fall, rise-fall and fall-rise. In particular, we are interested in the intonation pattern that takes place on the nucleus, where the biggest pitch variation takes place. For example, notice the main intonation pattern on this request which falls at the end:

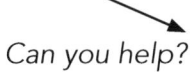

Can you help?

Now compare it with the rising intonation on the last syllable of this sentence, where the speaker is checking if the information is correct:

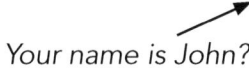

Your name is John?

The use of rise-fall and fall-rise intonation patterns is less common, and often used quite subtly to affect meaning. For example, to add emphasis to the exclamation 'Wow!', you might use a rise-fall pattern, though if applied very strongly it can imply sarcasm. Alternatively, a fall-rise intonation pattern over the word 'Sorry?' means 'What you just said was rather rude'.

6. Grammatical approach

When we are teaching and designing materials around pronunciation, we can use any of three different approaches to analyse intonation. **The grammatical approach** teaches intonation in the context of different aspects of grammar. For example, we might teach students that with *wh-* questions, the intonation will often fall at the end:

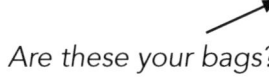

What time does he arrive?

… whereas with yes/no questions, the intonation often rises, like this:

Are these your bags?

Note that a grammatical approach is very prescriptive and rule-based; you will often find exceptions to the so-called 'rules', so consider the next two approaches.

7. Discoursal approach

If you take a discoursal approach to intonation, you are more concerned with the context of the sentence. For example, if we applied a grammatical approach to the question below, the rule or tendency would be that with *wh-* questions, the intonation falls. But in this case, the intonation pattern is fall-rise because the speaker has already discussed the person's arrival and wants to check the information:

What time does he arrive?

The discoursal approach is descriptive of what happens, whereas the grammatical approach is prescriptive.

8. Attitudinal approach

The approaches described in Tips 6 and 7 are concerned with the main intonation pattern, but our emotions or attitude in a situation will also affect the intonation. So the third **attitudinal approach** considers the **attitude** or **feelings** of the speaker, and how this affects intonation. It means that in class we might ask students to listen to a speaker and decide what the emotion of the speaker might be (for instance, angry, sad, happy, distrustful, uninterested, etc.).

9. Board work

There are different ways to show intonation, but the main consideration for the teacher is to choose one way and to be consistent when indicating it on the board. In many books on the subject, an intonation group is indicated with two slashes // and the intonation arrow is placed at the beginning.

// Can you help me?//

In published coursebooks the arrow is often placed over the nucleus or tail to show the main pattern at the end. Many teachers use the same system for their board work:

Can you help me?

You can also use a sweeping arrow over the whole sentence. This shows where the pitch rises on the head, continuing to the nucleus, and then the direction of movement after that:

I was wondering if you could help me?

10. To teach or not to teach intonation

Not all teachers believe in the value of formally teaching intonation. Some would argue that despite the idea that certain grammatical forms tend to have certain intonation, these are tendencies rather than rules and – as shown in Tip 7 – it is by no means fixed. Other teachers focus on raising students' awareness of how, for example, a speaker in a listening uses intonation to express meaning or to express certain emotions or attitude. The next unit provides a variety of ways to present and practise intonation. You can choose your preferred technique, depending on your viewpoint.

"It is now generally accepted that the best way to teach attitudinal intonation [in particular] is through exposure to authentic speech acts."

Sheila Thorn, author of *Integrating Authentic Listening into the Language Classroom* (2021, Pavilion Publishing and Media)

Unit 23

10 activities to present and practise intonation

Here are ten ideas for introducing intonation, making students aware of its tendencies, and encouraging them to try to apply it. You will also find more ideas for integrating intonation in Unit 27 (pages 85–87), Unit 29 (pages 91–93) and Units 31–32 (page 97–101).

1. Robot voice

One of the quickest ways to draw students' attention to intonation is to say the same phrase in two ways. Firstly, say it with very flat or bored-sounding intonation, perhaps in the style of a monotonous robot voice. Secondly, say it with normal or slightly exaggerated intonation. Then ask students what difference(s) they noticed. Encourage students in their own words to explain what they hear and notice.

2. Moving your hand

As you say a phrase with rising and falling intonation, move your outstretched hand from right to left in front of you (so students see it moving from their left-hand side to their right-hand side) as if your hand is passing over each part of the phrase. Raise your hand when the intonation rises and lower when the intonation falls. Invite students to do the same movement when drilling the phrase.

3. Up and down arrows

Each student takes two large pieces of paper or card and draws an up arrow (↑) on one and a down arrow (↓) on the other. Say a phrase or sentence. The students hold up the arrow that reflects the intonation at the end of the sentence. For example, with a statement like *See you tomorrow*, the intonation normally falls, so they will hold up the card showing the down arrow (↓). But we could also say *See you tomorrow?* as a way of checking if the other person wants to meet the next day. In this case, the intonation rises at the end, and students should hold up the card showing the up arrow (↑).

4. Intonation dictation

Dictate seven or eight short phrases that you have taught in class recently. Students listen and write them down. They then indicate if the intonation rise or falls at the end of each phrase by drawing an arrow over it. Be prepared to say your sentences a number of times. If you are concerned about saying them with the same intonation each time, record them before the class and play the recording.

5. Story beeps

Tell the students the start of a personal story. Choose one or two sentences from it. When you say these sentences, instead of saying the actual words, just say 'beep' for every word or syllable, paying specific attention to the intonation. The students work in groups to mark the intonation and then guess what the correct sentence was. Reveal the answer if they can't guess it. Then continue with the story until you come to the next sentence you have planned to highlight for intonation. Repeat the beeping task. For example:

It was a dark night. I went into the house and it was very scary. Suddenly, beep beep beep BEEP BEEP [rising intonation – There was a loud noise]. I turned around quickly. I couldn't see anything. I was shaking. BEEP beep beep BEEP? [rising intonation – What could it be?]

Unit 24

6. Humming

Another way to help students notice the intonation pattern on a phrase or sentence is to hum it so you don't use any words. By humming it, you allow students to focus on the intonation of the whole phrase or sentence. You can even write the words of the phrase on the board, hum it, and then have students repeat the phrase back to you, simultaneously applying the intonation pattern you hummed. This can often be much more effective – and memorable – than simply listening to and repeating the phrase.

Once students have become used to humming, they can have a go at doing it. Give each pair a different dialogue, like this:

A: Do you know where the pool is?

B: The swimming pool?

A: Yes. I want to go for a swim.

B: Just down this road on the left.

A: Next to the park?

B: Yes.

Each pair practises the dialogue without saying the actual words. They can add gestures and facial expressions, and hum the words, paying specific attention to stress and intonation. Finally, they perform it to the class. The other students try to guess the context, and if there's enough time, the actual dialogue.

7. How does the speaker sound or look?

Choose a short extract of video with close-ups of one or two speakers' faces. Find a highly emotional scene from a movie where the speaker has a particular look on their face as they speak. Play the video to the class with the sound off and ask students to guess how the speaker feels and what they might be saying. Then play the video with the sound on. Students listen closely to the intonation and think about what it tells us about the attitude of the speaker. Even if the level of English is high, students can still understand a great deal from the faces and the intonation.

Alternatively, play the video with the screen covered so that students can't see the characters, but they can hear the dialogue. Ask them to focus on the intonation rather than trying to understand every word. Students try predicting what the speakers look like and what emotions they are showing. Then play the video so they can see the screen and check their guesses.

8. Emotion adjectives

On the board, write a selection of emotion adjectives which your students already know, for instance, *happy, sad, angry, tired, bored, nervous*. Then invite a student to suggest a short sentence like: *I'm going to go out tonight*. Write it on the board. Next, choose one of the adjectives from the list on the board but don't tell the students which one. Say the sentence in the style of the adjective. Students have to guess the adjective. When you have modelled the activity a couple of times, ask a student to try it. Alternatively, you could put them into small groups for them to take turns saying the sentences in different ways.

Unit 24

9. Lists with rise, rise, rise, fall

When we list items, such as in a shopping list, we tend to use rising intonation on each item, until the last item on the end and the intonation falls. For instance:

For school, I need a book, a pen, a tablet, a coat, a dictionary, and a bag.

When you point out this tendency to students, explain that a rising intonation pattern like this often indicates that there is more information to follow. One way to practise this is to play a well-known ELT game where students sit in a circle. You begin by saying: *I'm starting an English course so I need a book, and a pen.* State two items in your list so you can model the rise on 'book' and fall on 'pen'. Then the first student repeats the sentence and has to think of and add a new item: *For school I need a book, a pen, and a tablet.* Make sure the student uses a rise, rise, fall intonation on the three items. Now it's the next student's turn. Each time, the new student has to remember all the items mentioned so far and then add a new one to the list. They also have to try and use the intonation pattern. Once the list becomes too long and impossible to remember, choose a new student to begin again and go round the circle in the same way. To add variety to the types of item listed, you can provide new sentence openers such as: *I'm cooking dinner tonight for friends so I need to buy … / I'm going on my summer holiday tomorrow so I need to pack … / I'm starting a new job tomorrow so I need … .*

10. How do you feel on a scale of 1 to 5?

Make copies of the 1 to 5 scales in Appendix 24.10 on page 167. Students work in A/B pairs. They receive one scale each. Give Student A four lines from a dialogue to read out. The dialogue could be taken from a listening you've recently used, or it could be a simple dialogue written on the board, such as: *Hello. How are you? Fine, thanks. And you? Not bad.*

For each line of the dialogue, Student A decides how they will feel on a scale of 1 to 5, where 1 is 'very sad' and 5 is 'very happy'. They circle the number on their scale. So, if they decide to sound very happy for *Hello*, they circle the number 5 on the first scale. Circling a 3 on the next line would indicate a 'so-so' mood for *How are you?* Next, Student A reads out the lines of the dialogue according to the emotion indicated on each scale line. Student B listens and circles the number they think Student A circled. At the end they compare, then swap roles.

"The important thing when teaching pronunciation – especially intonation – is to ham it up a bit and have some fun. You need to do that in order for learners to let their guard down."

Paul Dummett, teacher and author, Oxford, UK

Section 4:
Integrating pronunciation

Pronunciation is often taught in isolation, or in the form of a quick five-minute warm-up activity before moving on to grammar, vocabulary or the four skills of reading, writing, speaking and listening. But ideally, we should aim to integrate it, so it is taught alongside other aspects of language and language teaching.

This section explores a variety of ways to integrate pronunciation. It starts by looking at ways of integrating pronunciation in your grammar lessons. This will be especially helpful if you are using a coursebook which has lots of grammar practice but not much pronunciation.

Similarly, there are units to help you integrate pronunciation into lessons with vocabulary, including a focus on homophones and homographs. You will also find ideas for areas of language which pose specific pronunciation challenges such as sound–spelling differences, the alphabet, and delivering an effective presentation.

Many of the ideas presented throughout the book work with all age groups and in different contexts. For teachers of young learners, the section ends with a special unit containing tips for this age group.

10 ways to integrate more pronunciation into your lesson planning

Whenever you plan your lessons and study your coursebook in preparation for a lesson, it's always worth considering where and how you could add more pronunciation practice. Here are ten tips on how you might do this.

1. Lead-in photo

Many lessons (and coursebooks) start by showing students a photo to set the scene and to get them talking about a topic. If you plan on using this technique, think about the vocabulary students will need to describe the photo, and consider what pronunciation input or practice they will benefit from. For example, are there any words where you will need to highlight the word stress?

In the case of the photo below, the topic was 'Shopping', and the teacher began the lesson by showing this photo. They explained it was a barber's shop, and then asked the students to work out the pronunciation pun in the title of the shop on the photo. The difference between the words *shop* and *chop* drew attention to the sounds ʃɒp and tʃɒp and provided an engaging way into the topic of shops.

2. Dictation

If you are using any kind of short text in a lesson, you can dictate it first before students read it. Dictation is excellent listening practice; it draws attention to the pronunciation of words. After you have dictated the text two or three times, show students the correct text (either on the board or in their coursebook). They can compare what they heard and wrote down with the original.

3. Read the text aloud

When you use a reading text with your students, you could read the text aloud to the class. They listen and read. It's a useful way for them to notice sound–spelling differences. Afterwards, students could also try reading the text quietly on their own. (See Unit 32, pages 100–101.)

4. Listening

After an extended listening task, try to isolate certain sentences from the recording which illustrate certain pronunciation features; for example, you might choose two or three sentences with plenty of connected speech. Write the sentences on the board and play them from the recording. Have students mark the stressed words or draw the link between certain sounds. (See Unit 22, pages 67–70.)

5. Vocabulary notebooks

If you encourage your students to keep a vocabulary notebook with different information about new words from the lesson, you could give them a copy of the example in Appendix 25.5 on page 168. Make sure they notice how the student includes information about pronunciation and encourage them to do the same.

6. Grammar

When teaching grammar, consider any pronunciation features that relate to the form; the most common example will be that of contracted forms with auxiliary verbs, such as *I'm, it's, isn't, don't, doesn't*, etc. Spend a little time drilling the form or focusing on its features. (See Unit 8, pages 31–33, and Unit 27, pages 85–87.)

7. Speaking

When preparing students for a speaking activity such as a role-play or discussion, it is helpful to pre-teach useful phrases that they will need to use. For example, for a discussion, you might teach functional language for expressing and asking for opinions, such as *What do you think? I agree with … I disagree with ….* When introducing such phrases, first drill them with the whole class and then individually. There is more chance students will use these phrases if you have focused on how, as well as when, to say them. (See Unit 8, pages 31–33.)

8. Error correction

During a speaking activity with the focus on fluency, monitor the students' language and remember to note down any pronunciation difficulties they have with pronunciation as well as any other language point. Don't forget to include a few minutes in your lesson plan to give feedback on what the students said well, and what they need to improve on.

9. Review language from the lesson

Try setting aside five minutes at the end of the lesson to review any new language from the lesson and to check students can pronounce it. If you have listed all the new vocabulary in a column on the board (see Unit 29, pages 91–93), you can quickly drill the class and check everyone knows the pronunciation. Another fun ending to a lesson is to play 'Pass it on' with the new language. It works like this: Divide the students into groups of six. You give one student in the group one of the new words from the lesson. That student whispers the word to the person on their left. That person then whispers the word they think they heard to the person on their left. This whispering goes round the circle until it arrives at the sixth person, who says the word aloud. The group can see if everyone said and heard it correctly and also – if the word has changed – the group can guess why someone might have misheard the pronunciation in some way.

10. Your lesson plan

You are probably familiar with the idea of a formal lesson plan. Many language schools ask teachers to fill them in, and on training courses leading to qualifications, filling in a formal plan is a course requirement. Although you probably don't write a formal plan for every lesson, it's worth doing so from time to time as lesson plans make you re-assess the way you approach a lesson. For the purposes of integrating pronunciation into your next lesson, why not add a column for pronunciation and consider how and when you could integrate more pronunciation into a lesson? Try organising each stage of your lesson plan like this:

Stage and aim	Procedure	Additional pronunciation	Timing

"Pronunciation work is much more effective being integrated into meaningful practice. That way learners can build up their knowledge purposefully and recognise spoken phonological features as they listen rather than getting tied up in the detail of what they think they 'should' produce or sounds in isolation."

Kirsten Holt, head of Pavilion ELT at Pavilion Publishing, UK

10 ways to integrate pronunciation with the tenses

When teaching the present and past tenses and future forms, it's important to integrate some of the pronunciation points below. Alternatively, you might have already presented the tenses; if this is the case, you can present key pronunciation which also allows you to revise the forms. As well as the key pronunciation areas of teaching the present tenses (tips 1–2), past tenses (tips 3–8) and future forms (tips 9–10), you'll also find ideas for activities.

1. Present simple and s, z and ɪz phonetic endings

Words ending in -s can be pronounced **s**, **z** or **ɪz**, so the following pronunciation rules can also be taught with plural forms. However, it is often taught as part of the present simple because of the -s endings added to the *he/she/it forms*. One way to demonstrate the difference is to offer students groups of verbs where they all have the same -s ending sounding except one of them. Read them aloud; students have to guess the odd verb out:

1. *finishes, decides, dances, watches, promises* (They all end with **ɪz**, except *decides*, which ends with **z**.)

2. *plays, plans, gives, starts, goes* (They all end with **z**, except *starts*, which ends with **s**.)

3. *hopes, speaks, moves, wants, waits* (They all end with **s**, except *moves*, which ends with **z**.)

Students can also listen to all the verbs again and try to work out the rule. Alternatively, they can try to establish which types of sounds come before the -s endings. For example, in the lists above, the sounds **ʃ**, **s** and **tʃ** come before **ɪz**. In 2, any vowel sound, **n** and **v** are before **z**. In 3, **p**, **k** and **t** come before **s**.

2. Continuous forms with ŋ endings

For any words ending in *-ing*, you will need to help students with the **ŋ** sound. It's helpful to do this when teaching continuous forms (present, past or future). Try to demonstrate to students how the back of the tongue rests on the soft palate at the back of the mouth. Some teachers do this with their hands: one hand represents the top of the mouth and the other hand represents the shape of the tongue. An **articulators of speech diagram** is also useful for this (see Appendix 9, page 151). Also, encourage them to hear how the sound is nasal – they should feel their nose vibrate a little.

3. Regular past simple and the extra syllable ɪd

When we introduce students to regular verbs in the past simple, we explain that you add the letters -ed (or -d) to the verb; for example, *play* ➜ *played*, *want* ➜ *wanted*, *dance* ➜ *danced*. Draw their attention to the fact that when you add -ed or -d, the number of syllables sometimes stays the same: *play* = 1 syllable and *played* = 1 syllable. But with some regular verbs, adding -ed means you are adding an extra syllable: *want* = 1 syllable but *wanted* = 2 syllables (the -ed ending is pronounced **ɪd**). So, when introducing the verbs in the past simple, ask students how many syllables they hear. Alternatively, give them a selection of verbs like this and ask them to categorise them into two groups: 1. 'no extra syllable' and 2. 'one extra syllable'. Once they have grouped them, ask if they can guess the rule. (The rule: when the infinitive form ends in a **t** or **d** sound, the -ed ending is an extra syllable.)

> played   wanted   danced   hoped   waited   decided   climbed   helped

(Answers: 1. *played, danced, hoped, climbed, helped*. 2. *wanted, waited, decided*)

ETpedia: Pronunciation © Pavilion Publishing and Media Ltd and its licensors 2022.

4. Regular past simple and phonemes: t, d, ɪd

Following on from 1, in which some past simple verbs have the extra syllable **ɪd**, you might also have students notice that when you add *-ed* to certain verbs without creating an extra syllable, the end consonant sound can either be a **t** or **d** sound. For example, the *-ed* in *played* is a **d** sound, whereas the *-ed* in *helped* is a **t** sound. Not all teachers agree that this is a necessary distinction for students to be able to hear or produce – you can decide what's best your learners. If you do want to draw attention to it, read out a set of verbs such as those listed in Tip 1, and have students write them into a table like this:

d	t	ɪd
played	danced	wanted
climbed	hoped	waited
	helped	decided

If you want to teach a rule for the **d** and **t** sound, point out that **d** follows a verb ending with a voiced consonant and the **t** sound follows a verb with an unvoiced consonant. (See Unit 18, pages 56–58 on voiced and unvoiced sounds.)

5. Irregular verbs in the past

One of the biggest challenges for students when using past forms is memorising the forms of irregular verbs such as *go–went–gone*. Part of memorising them involves getting to grips with the pronunciation. Many coursebooks include verb tables in the reference section listing the most common irregular verbs in their three forms. You can also use the **irregular verb list** in Appendix 26.5 on page 169. When students try to memorise these lists, encourage them to listen to the forms being spoken. One way you can help is to make a recording of these lists for them to listen to at home.

6. Analysing a verb table

Following on from Tip 5, use the verb table in your coursebook or the list in Appendix 26.5 on page 169 and ask students to answer these three questions about the vowel sounds in the verb forms:

1. Which irregular verb has vowel sounds that change in every form?

2. Which irregular verb has vowel sounds that are the same in two forms?

3. Which vowel sounds are the same for all three forms?

For example, for question 1, a correct answer would be *swim–swam–swum*, where the three vowel sounds are ɪ, æ and ʌ. For question 2, a correct answer would be *bring–brought–brought* because the two past forms share the same vowel sound ɔ:. And for question 3, although there is a spelling change with *build–built–built*, the vowel sound ɪ in the middle stays the same for all three forms.

Unit 26

7. Past participles

This activity shows how certain past participle forms have the same vowel sounds. Write the following verbs on the board in their infinitive form and ask students to write their past participle form.

> win   buy   show   run   think   throw   do   bring   teach   fly   swim   grow

Check what students have written as past participles (they should have written *won*, *bought*, *shown*, *run*, *thought*, *thrown*, *done*, *brought*, *taught*, *flown*, *swum*, *grown*). Then ask them to group the past participles by vowel sound in the table below. Put the first three at the top of each column and/or write the vowel phoneme if students are familiar with it.

1. won ʌ	2. bought ɔː	3. shown əʊ

(Answer key: 1. won, run, done, swum 2. bought, thought, brought, taught 3. shown, thrown, flown, grown)

8. Past participles crossword

For further practice with irregular verbs in the past, make copies of the crossword page in Appendix 26.8 on page 170 for every two students. Cut the page in half and assign one half to Student A and one to Student B. The aim is to complete the crossword with past participle forms. Each student has half of the verbs in the past simple form; the answers are past participles in the crossword. Students take turns to ask the questions, for example, *What is 3 across?* or *What is 1 down?* The partner answers with the past simple form and then the student who asked the question says and writes the past participle form in the crossword. As students complete the activity, make sure they are saying the words aloud as well as writing them in the crossword. (Note that you can increase the challenge by cutting off the clues. Each student has to work out the past simple forms based on the past participles in their crossword. Then they start the speaking activity.)

9. Connected speech for *going to*

From an early stage in their learning, students are taught that 'going to' is used for talking about future plans and future intentions. They soon notice that many speakers say it as ˈgənə rather than as ˈgəʊɪŋ tuː. Sometimes, students comment that this kind of pronunciation is the American English way of saying *going to*, when in fact it's just as commonly used in everyday British English. Most students like trying to say *going to* in this way, so once you have built up a selection of sentences using the 'going to' form, students can try saying them with ˈgənə. (See Unit 22, pages 67–70.)

10. Light and dark L sounds with *will* and *'ll*

With future forms, students don't normally have too many problems pronouncing the word *will* **wɪl** but given that it is usually contracted to *'ll* **l**, students need to be aware of its use, and most will want to try and incorporate it into their own speech. You may want to use this as an opportunity to focus on the difference between what are often referred to as the 'light L' and the 'dark L' sounds. A 'light L' is when the **l** sound comes at the beginning of a word and so the tip of the tongue touches the back of the top teeth and moves forward, as in the word 'light'. A 'dark L' sound is when the **l** sound comes at the end of the word, as in *will* or *'ll* and the tip of the tongue lands on the alveolar ridge. In fact, the key reason for spending time on this sound is not so students produce it but because they need to hear it and recognise when the speaker refers to the present or the future. Because the *'ll* sound is dark, students often don't hear it. That might lead them to assume that the sentence is in the present simple (for instance, talking about routines), and not about the future. You could read aloud the sentences below at normal speed. Ask students if the sentence refers to the present or the future.

I go to school. (present)	*I'll go to school.* (future)
They'll call you back. (future)	*They call me at midday.* (present)
We live in this house. (present)	*We'll live here.* (future)
Prices'll go up again. (future)	*Prices go down in January.* (present)

"When using a video, in order to help students develop decoding skills, I make gap-filling activities in which students have to listen for function words (ie. auxiliary verbs, modals, prepositions, pronouns, etc.) rather than content words (main verbs, adjectives, nouns, ...) because, most of the times, the former are unstressed, yet more difficult to decode."

Silvina Mascitti, teacher and materials writer at eflcreativeideas.com

Unit 26

10 ways to integrate pronunciation with grammar

When we present grammar items in a lesson, we usually cover the form, meaning and use. But we often omit aspects of pronunciation which occur with certain areas of grammar. In this unit, we look at ten aspects of grammar which tend to have certain pronunciation features. They will give you ideas for encouraging students to listen out for them, and possibly also to reproduce them when speaking.

1. Pronouns

Right from the beginning of an English course, new students have to cope with learning a range of pronouns and the verb *to be*. After you have introduced them in the first few lessons, it's worth reviewing them by writing these pairs of words on the board, reading them aloud, and asking students to identify which have the same pronunciation:

1. *your – you're* (same/different)
2. *he's – his* (same/different)
3. *it's – its* (same/different)
4. *our – are* (same/different)
5. *theirs – there's* (same/different)
6. *they're – their* (same/different)
7. *this – these* (same/different)

(Answers: Note that there may be some variation depending on the accent of the recording voice or your own accent: 1. same 2. different 3. same 4. different 5. same 6. same 7. different.)

2. Indefinite articles: *a* and *an*

The indefinite article is introduced at beginner level. Almost immediately, there is the pronunciation issue that you use *a* before a word starting with a consonant sound (*a teacher, a manager*) but you have to use *an* before a word starting with a vowel sound (*an engineer, an accountant*). The simplest way to practise this rule is to give students a list of nouns and ask them to decide whether they use *a* or *an* before the words. To do this, students need to understand the difference between a **consonant** sound and a **vowel** sound, so even at lower levels, it's good moment to introduce these two terms.

3. Definite article: *the*

There are two ways we pronounce *the*. When it is used before a word starting with a consonant sound, such as 'the bee', it is pronounced with the schwa sound: **ðə**. But if the word that follows it starts with a vowel sound, as in 'the ant', it's pronounced **ði:**. In addition, there is a linking **j** sound between the two words, like this: **ði:jænt**. Arguably, it won't affect intelligibility if students can't reproduce this difference and add the intrusive **j** sound when speaking, but the more they listen to the authentic speech of certain speakers, the more they will hear this feature, so it's worth drawing their attention to it, perhaps at intermediate levels and above.

4. *can* and *can't*

When introducing *can* at lower levels for the first time, you might want to draw students' attention to the fact that the letter '*a*' in this modal verb often changes depending on its use (especially in British English), like this:

ETpedia: Pronunciation © Pavilion Publishing and Media Ltd and its licensors 2022.

kæn in questions and short answers (*Can you sing? Yes, I can.*)

kɑːnt in the negative (*I can't sing.*)

kən in affirmative sentences (*I can sing.*)

Once you have presented these three differences, read out a few sentences with *can* or *can't*. Ask students to try and notice the difference. They can write down the phoneme for the sound they hear. Alternatively, have them make three cards, each with one phoneme: **æ**, **ɑː** and **ə**, and get them to hold up the phoneme they hear in each sentence. This is also a very fast way for you to know what they are hearing.

5. Comparative forms

When introducing comparative forms, it's useful to highlight sentence stress and show how the comparative adjective is stressed and other words around it are unstressed, like this:

CARS are FASTer than BIKES.

TRUCKS are BIGGer than CARS.

BIKES are CLEANer than PLANES.

Notice also that a set of sentences like this has a natural rhythm. If you say them one after the other, you can have fun creating chants.

6. Prepositions of time, place and movement

Because so many prepositions tend to start with a vowel sound (*in, on, at, up, onto, into, along, across*), they are often linked to the word that precedes them. When students listen to everyday speech, they may find this aspect of connected speech challenging; for example, notice the linking in these sentences:

It **starts‿at** three.

The picture **is‿on** the wall.

In addition, with prepositions of movement which follow verbs like *go*, intrusion will also occur; for example, *go‿w‿in, go‿w‿up*. As you introduce this area of grammar, spend some time drawing attention to the linking, and drill some of the chunks of language containing the prepositions.

7. *use to, used to, used*

When teaching *used to* + verb for talking about past habits, situations or states, we normally draw attention to the fact that you don't hear the letter *d* in *used to*; it sounds similar to the *use to* in the negative and question form. However, when you say the verb to *use* in the past simple, you hear the **d** sound at the end, and the letter *s* has a **z** sound instead of a **s** sound. To illustrate this for students, read these sentences aloud and ask them to spot the similarities and differences in the pronunciation of *use* and *used*. Then write the phonemic script afterwards if your students are familiar with it.

I **used** to drive a car.	**juːs**
I didn't **use** to drive a car.	**juːs**
Did you **use** to drive a car?	**juːs**
I **used** your car.	**juːzd**
I didn't **use** your car.	**juːz**
Did you **use** my car?	**juːz**

8. *have to*

For saying that we 'have to' do something, *have to* would be transcribed with the **v** phoneme: **'hæv tʊ**. However, in everyday speech, the **v** becomes a **f** sound and the *to* is unstressed, so the two words sound closely joined: **hæftə**. Again, it may not matter whether students can pronounce it as **hæftə** but they should be aware that they will often hear it said like that in everyday conversation, and it's worth pointing it out when it occurs in any recorded listening that you play.

9. Relative clauses

We often introduce defining and non-defining relative clauses with intermediate-level students. Non-defining relative clauses, which provide extra but not essential information, are enclosed by commas. These commas indicate where it's natural to pause. When indicating this feature on the board, you can use this symbol (/) to indicate pauses. You could also highlight that the intonation tends to rise on the stressed syllable before the commas, like this:

My sister / who lives in New Zealand / is visiting me next week.

It's an easy pronunciation point to learn because it reflects the punctuation and is helpful for students who have to give more formal talks and presentations (see Unit 35, pages 108–110).

10. Conditionals

Focusing on contracted forms in conditionals is particularly important because they can contain a number of verb forms which are usually contracted such as *will* ('*ll*), *had* ('*d*), *would* ('*d*) and *have* ('*ve*). One activity you can do to practise this is to write some conditional sentences on the board and ask students to circle any words which could be contracted. Then say the sentences aloud or play a recording of them so students can hear if their guesses are correct. For example, here are three sentences you could use with the contracted forms shown in brackets:

If I leave now, I will arrive at two. (I'll)

If you left now, you would arrive at two. (you'd)

If you had left then, you would have arrived by two. (you'd left; you'd've arrived)

If you decide to drill these contracted forms in conditional sentences, it's worth chunking the drill so students only attempt parts of the sentence to start with. For example, with the challenging *you'd've arrived*, it would be worth building up the drill step by step like this:

you'd ...

you'd've ...

you'd've arrived ...

you'd've arrived by two ...

(See Unit 8, pages 31–33 for more tips on drilling pronunciation.)

In addition to the contracted forms in conditionals, you could also mark and practise the rise-and-fall intonation arrows that are typical of conditional sentences with the two clauses:

If I leave now, I will arrive at two.

Unit 27

10 tendencies and activities for asking questions

Given how often we teach question forms and encourage students to ask questions in class, it makes sense that we should use these opportunities to focus on the pronunciation tendencies of questions, in particular on the suprasegmental features of intonation, sentence stress and connected speech. You can teach these pronunciation features either at the time of introducing a question form or separately, so that you review the question forms in a new way.

1. Rising intonation with yes/no questions

One tendency in English (not an absolute rule) is for the intonation on yes/no questions to rise at the end like this:

Do you come from Spain?

So when you introduce this type of question form with a beginner or elementary level class, it's relatively simple to integrate this aspect of intonation into the lesson.

2. Falling intonation with *wh-* questions

Following on from Tip 1, whereas the intonation tends to rise on yes/no questions, it generally falls on *wh-* questions, like this:

Where do you come from?

It often makes sense to teach this tendency alongside the rising intonation on yes/no questions so that students can contrast them. Or, if you have played a recording of people asking questions, play it again and have students notice the intonation patterns they use.

3. Falling and rising intonation on question tags

Students find question tags notoriously difficult because the rules for matching the auxiliary verb in the tag are tricky. In addition, the intonation on the tag can greatly affect the speaker's meaning.

When the intonation falls, the speaker is fairly certain and just wants to confirm the information:

You're from Spain, aren't you?

In contrast, rising intonation on a question tag indicates that the speaker is uncertain and genuinely wants to find out the answer, like this:

You're from Madrid, aren't you?

To raise your students' awareness of the two intonation patterns in 3 and 4, you could read out a series of questions with tags, using a falling or rising intonation. Students indicate if they heard a rise or fall. (See **Up and down arrows** in Unit 24.3, page 74 for an activity to practise further.)

Unit 28

4. How well do you know each other?

Following on from Tips 2 and 3, this activity provides freer practice using question tags. Put the students into pairs so they are working with another student that they know reasonably well. Individually, each student writes five things that they know are definitely true and that they think might be true about their partner, for instance, their surname, nationality, age, free-time interests, etc. When they are ready with their five pieces of information, they read them to their partner using question tags to either confirm the information (with falling intonation) or to check if it's correct (with rising intonation). For example:

A: Your surname is Braun, isn't it?   **B:** Yes, it is.

A: You're 21, aren't you?   **B:** No, I'm not. I'm 20.

5. Stressing the question word

One feature of asking questions is stressing the first question word when we want to show surprise about the answer or to check we understood. For instance:

A: How much did your coat cost?

B: A hundred dollars.

A: HOW much did it cost?

A fun way to practise this feature is to have students imagine they have been shopping and bought a new item. They write four or five statements about their shopping trip. When they are ready, they work in pairs and read out each sentence. Their partner is very nosy and has to create a question for the sentence, stressing the first word to show surprise. So they might create conversations like this:

A: I went shopping in Paris.

B: WHERE did you go shopping?

A: In Paris. I bought a painting.

B: WHAT did you buy?

A: A painting. Picasso painted it.

B: WHO painted it?

A: Picasso. It cost five million dollars.

B: HOW much did it cost?

etc ...

6. Turning statements into questions

Show students that in informal conversation, statements can be turned into questions. Write a few short statements on the board. Say them with falling intonation and then repeat them with rising intonation to show how the speaker is asking a question. For instance, in these examples the teacher is presenting statements in the context of offering a guest something to eat and drink:

You want a sandwich.   *Cheese and lettuce is OK.*

A drink with that.   *You like coke.*

By adding rising intonation to each one, you are asking a question, for example:

You want a sandwich?

Unit 28

7. Complete conversations with statements as questions

Following on from Tip 6, have students turn four statements into a complete conversation with responses as shown below. After students have written the conversation in full, they practise it in pairs, with Student A using rising intonation on the statements:

A:	You want a sandwich?		**B:**	Yes, please.
A:	Cheese and lettuce is OK.		**B:**	That's fine.
A:	You'd like a drink?		**B:**	That'd be nice.
A:	You like coke?		**B:**	Not really. I prefer water.

8. Offers and requests

With offers and requests starting with *Would you like …?* and *Could I have …?*, the sounds in the phrases are often reduced or even disappear from the full forms **wʊd jʊ laɪk** and **kʊd aɪ hæv** to the reduced forms of **wʊdʒə laɪk** and **kʊdehəv**. So when you play a recording of conversations with offers and requests (for example, in a shop), draw students' attention to this feature. And when students role-play similar situations involving offers and requests, let them try using these reduced phrases and notice the difference compared to the full forms.

9. Connected speech questions in songs

In everyday spoken English, many questions are asked with connected speech. For example, it's common to hear a question like *What are you going to do?* which sounds like *Wotcha gonna do?* Sometimes, this way of asking a question becomes so common that it is even written down this way. Good examples of this language feature come from pop songs so it can be fun to write the title of the song on the board and then play part of it. Ask students to read and listen, and then to try and write the title in full. Here are four songs you could use (with the full form of the written question shown afterwards):

What'cha Gonna Do About It? by the Small Faces (*What are you going to do about it?*)

Whatcha say? by Jason Derulo (*What did you say?*)

Could'ya (fall in love with me)? by Nat King Cole (*Could you fall in love with me?*)

Are you gonna go my way? by Lenny Kravitz (*Are you going to go my way?*)

10. Sing along with a song

Following on from using songs in the previous activity, there are also song titles which use questions written in full, but when you listen to the singer, they illustrate the effect of connected speech. Students often like to join in, trying to say the question with connected speech. Three good examples to use are:

Could you be loved by Bob Marley (in which Bob Marley sings *Could'ja be, could'ja be, could'ja a be loved ….*).

Who are you? by The Who (in which Roger Daltrey clearly demonstrates the intrusive **w** sound between *who* and *are*).

Should I stay or should I go? by The Clash (in which Joe Strummer demonstrates the linking between *should* and *I*).

Unit 28

10 ways to integrate pronunciation with vocabulary

Many course syllabuses and coursebooks include a list of vocabulary areas to be taught, but they may be lacking in pronunciation items to teach. Perhaps this is because it's assumed that when you teach the vocabulary, you will naturally teach the pronunciation of that word. Many of the tips and ideas in the previous units have prepared you for teaching vocabulary. However, the aim of this unit is to highlight how you can integrate particular areas of pronunciation when certain vocabulary is taught.

1. Content words

Content words are the words that carry the main meaning in a text; they mainly include verbs, nouns, adjectives and adverbs. These are the types of words that will often get you what you want in a foreign language, even if you are at a very low level, because they communicate the main meaning; for example, a beginner-level student who walks into a café and says, *Two, coffee, please* will probably be understood. However, for many other situations, the speaker will also need what are called 'function words'. These auxiliary verbs, prepositions, conjunctions, pronouns and determiners add structure to the language. The relevance to pronunciation is that in a sentence we tend to stress the content words and unstress the function words. So, when teaching new vocabulary and its part of speech, we are in effect saying whether it's a content or a function word, and so indicating if it's likely to be stressed or unstressed. This is of particular importance to students for listening because the content words are much easier to hear than the function words.

2. Word forms

When teaching the different forms of a word, remember that the word stress might stay the same or it might change. When students record the different forms of a root word like *present*, it's important that they get into the habit of also recording the stressed syllable like this: *pre<u>sent</u>* (verb), *pre<u>sent</u>able* (adjective), *<u>pre</u>sent* (noun), *pre<u>sent</u>er* (person) *presen<u>ta</u>tion* (noun).

3. Suffixes and prefixes

Whenever you teach prefixes and suffixes, the quick and easy rule is to tell students that these are never stressed in a word. For example, here are two words, one with the prefix *un-* and one with the suffix *-al*; those are not the stressed syllables: *un<u>ambi</u>tious*, *infor<u>ma</u>tional*. The exception to this rule might be when a speaker needs to stress the prefix, perhaps for clarification, as in this exchange:

A: I'm really ambitious.

B: Sorry did you say you were <u>un</u>ambitious?!!

A: No, I said I am <u>am</u>bitious, not <u>un</u>ambitious.

You can make this feature part of a lesson by having students write a similar dialogue in which the word and the word with a prefix both appear and are stressed in the same way as in the exchange above.

4. Compound nouns

Normally, the first word in a compound noun has the main stress. Here are some examples you could use to demonstrate this: *<u>brief</u>case, <u>mine</u>ral water, <u>junk</u> food, <u>cli</u>mate change*.

5. Numbers

It can be challenging for learners to get to grips with the way we say and pronounce numbers in English, and the longer the number, or if it includes features such as decimal places or symbols, the more difficult it is knowing how to say them. Initially, there is the problem that numbers in the teens can be easily confused with numbers ending in -ty. So it's worth teaching students who deal with numbers a lot (especially over the phone) how to clarify the difference using the technique of stressing the second syllable, like this:

A: The price is nineteen thousand.

B: Sorry did you say nine<u>teen</u> or <u>nine</u>ty?

A: Nine<u>teen</u>.

In addition, there are other things students need to know about pronouncing numbers such as fractions, and numbers denoting lengths and temperatures. To help deal with these, you can make copies of the simple matching exercise for students in Appendix 29.4, which includes an answer key with explanations.

(Answers 1. h) 2. a) 3. j) 4. b) 5. c) 6. i) 7. d) 8. f) 9. g) 10. e))

6. Phrasal verbs

In phrasal verbs, the particle is usually stressed more than the main verb. So if you say any of these phrasal verbs in a complete sentence, you'll notice that the underlined particle is stressed more than the main verb:

log <u>in</u> (to a computer)

look <u>up</u> (a word in a dictionary)

get <u>up</u> (in the morning)

hang <u>out</u> (with friends)

One interesting feature you could mention to higher-level students is that when these phrasal verbs are turned into nouns, the stress shifts like this:

I need to log <u>in</u> to my computer ➜ *What are the <u>log</u>in details for this computer?*

Let's hang <u>out</u> in this café for a while. ➜ *This café is one of my favourite <u>hang</u>outs.*

The other pronunciation feature that is important to draw attention to with phrasal verbs is the linking that often occurs between the two words because the main verbs often end in a consonant sound and the participle often starts with a vowel sound. In natural speech, the two words can sound like one: *log‿in, look‿up, get‿up, hang‿out.*

7. Plurals

For plural nouns ending in -s, the sound of the final -s can be **s** or **z**, or an additional syllable is added with the **IZ** sound, as shown in the three columns below:

s	z	IZ
shorts	clothes	glasses
books	phones	classes
cups	bags	

Unit 29

One fun way to get students standing up and moving around at the end of a long lesson is to display pieces of paper with the three phonemes in different parts of the classroom. You call out plural nouns and students run to the symbol they think is correct for the -s ending.

8. Binomials

Binomials are often formally taught at upper-intermediate levels, but students will have met them very early on at elementary levels such as: *give and take, come and go, peace and quiet, back to front, all or nothing, sooner or later*. Binomials are fixed expressions with two words (often nouns) which are joined by a conjunction (most commonly and). As a result, binomials have a natural rhythm of STRESS unstress STRESS. Probably the most famous example of a binomial is *rock 'n' roll*, which even reflects the pronunciation pattern by omitting the letters a and d from the unstressed conjunction. *Fish 'n' chips* is another well-known example. One fun activity is to write on the board these binomials which you might hear used in a café situation. Have students work in pairs and write a dialogue using all four (and more if they can think of some):

tea or coffee   milk and sugar   one or two   black or white

Before students start reading their dialogues aloud, you can point out that we often use a rise–fall intonation on binomials when we use them as questions, like this:

Tea or coffee? = Would you like tea or coffee?

9. Collective nouns, quantities and amounts

When teaching students how to turn uncountable nouns into countable nouns, we often show them the a ... of ... structure, as in *a slice of cake, a bag of rice, a tin of peas, a bunch of flowers*. But fewer teachers also take this opportunity to highlight the sentence stress pattern that naturally occurs because the words a and of are unstressed. In addition, there is normally linking between the consonant sound at the end of the first noun and the word *of*. So, visually, you can show the pattern like this and have students listen and repeat:

a SLICE‿of CAKE

a BAG‿of RICE

a TIN‿of PEAS

a BUNCH‿of FLOWers

10. Similes

Similes using the comparative *as ... as* form have a similar pattern to that shown in Tip 9, and so it's worth introducing it when you work on this vocabulary area which is normally taught at intermediate level. The *as ... as* words are unstressed and the other words are stressed. Linking also naturally occurs as shown here:

as BLIND‿as‿a BAT

as BUSY‿as‿a BEE

as GOOD‿as GOLD

as WHITE‿as SNOW

ETpedia: Pronunciation © Pavilion Publishing and Media Ltd and its licensors 2022.

10 ideas for homophones and homographs

There is an obvious spelling challenge for students when they come across words which are homophones and homographs. Often you will come across a new homophone unexpectedly in a lesson because a student is confused by the identical pronunciation but different spelling of two words like *for* and *four*. Or, when students read the word *minute* in a text, they can be forgiven for thinking it refers to a measurement of time and is pronounced **mɪnɪt**, when in fact it describes something very small and is pronounced **maɪˈnjuːt**.

1. Homophones

Homophones are words which are spelt differently but pronounced the same way, such as: *aloud/allowed, bare/bear, be/bee, brake/break, dear/deer, eye/I, for/four, flew/flu, grate/great, hear/here, hour/our, its/it's, know/no, mail/male, meat/meet, one/won, pair/pear, practise/practise* (UK English), *red/read, roll/role, sail/sale, some/sum, steal/steel, their/there, through/threw, to/too, way/weigh, weak/week, wear/where, whether/weather, write/right, wood/would.*

2. Homographs

Homographs have the same spelling but are pronounced differently, so the word close in these two sentences is pronounced in two different ways: *I'm very close to my brother. / Can you close the door?* Other common examples of homographs are *lead, live, minute, read, refuse, row, tear, use* and *wind.*

3. Level

As you can see from the examples given in Tips 1 and 2 above, homophones such as *be/bee* appear at low levels (**CEFR** A1 and A2), so you will need to draw students' attention to them early on in their learning. There are also quite a few homographs that become more noticeable at higher levels. So a students will have learnt the verb *close* as in *close the door* at elementary level (A1), but will then meet the homograph *close* as in *I'm close to my brother* at intermediate level (B1) before also learning that the C2-level noun *close* can also mean *end*, as in *at the close of play* (in a cricket match, for example).

4. Contextualise

When you and your students notice a homophone in a lesson, it's worth focusing on the meaning by writing the two words in different sentences on the board. Another way to make it memorable is to use the words in the same sentence like this: *There must be a bee in here!* You could even give students a set of five homophones and ask them to try and write five sentences with the pairs of words. The same exercise is possible with homographs, though much harder, for instance, *I refuse to take out my refuse!*

Unit 30

5. Distinguishing homophones

A simple distinguishing activity with homophones is to show students the two words side by side and read out one sentence with one of the words. Students have to choose which word they think they heard. For example, for these three pairs, write them on the board and then read the following sentences aloud:

aloud – allowed   hear – here   weak – week

1. *We're not allowed inside at lunch.*

2. *Can you hear me?*

3. *I feel very weak today.*

(Answers: 1. allowed 2. hear 3. weak)

6. Distinguishing homographs

You can do a similar activity as that described in Tip 5 with homographs if your students are familiar with phonemic script like this:

kləʊz – kləʊs   lɪv – laɪv   teə(r) – tɪə(r)

1. *Please <u>close</u> the door behind you.*

2. *U2 are playing <u>live</u> at the stadium tonight.*

3. *You have a <u>tear</u> in your eye.*

(Answers: 1. **kləʊz** 2. **laɪv** 3. **tɪə(r)**)

7. Spot the mistake

Write a selection of sentences using homophones. Make the spelling in some sentences correct and make a mistake with the homophone in others. Students read the sentences aloud, underline the homophone and decide if it is correct or not. For example:

1. How much do you *way*? (Incorrect: *weigh*)

2. I *threw* the ball to her. (Correct)

3. I've *red* this book five times. (Incorrect: *read*)

4. Do you know the answer to this *sum*? (Correct)

5. I'd like an apple and a *pair*. (Incorrect: *pear*)

8. Underline the correct homophone

For lower levels, a simple way to help students identify the correct homophone is to give them a choice and they underline the correct word, like this:

1. *It's/Its* mine, not yours.

2. We've been here for *ours/hours*.

3. Do you *no/know* the address?

(Answers: 1. It's 2. hours 3. know)

9. Write a dialogue with homographs

With higher levels, put students in pairs and give each pair a different homograph. Students write a short dialogue set in any situation, but the dialogue must make use of the homograph twice with its different pronunciation and meaning. When students have completed their dialogues, they perform them to the class and the other students must listen and identify the homographs used. For example, if the homograph is *row*, the conversation might be:

A: Here's our boat. Can I *row*?

B: Oh! I wanted to do it.

A: But you did it last time.

B: I did not! You did.

A: OK, let's not have a *row* about it. You go first and then I'll do it.

B: Agreed!

10. Homophone pelmanism

Make copies of Appendix 30.10 on page 172 and cut up the words so that you have enough sets for groups of three to four players. The words are designed so that each homophone will match another homophone and each homograph will match two different words, depending on how you pronounce it. Players shuffle the cards and place them face down in the middle of a table. Players take turns to turn over two cards until one player finds two cards with words which have matching sounds, for instance, *need* = *read* or *fed* = *read*. If they match two words correctly, they keep them and have another turn. The winner is the player who matches the most pairs of words.

"Pronunciation can often go unnoticed in the language classroom, which is why bringing it to students' attention and documenting their progress are key. Giving them evidence of their progress by recording them when reading [aloud]/speaking at the start, middle and end of your school year will increase their motivation and self-confidence."

Dr Christina Nicole Giannikas, education and research consultant, Cyprus

10 ideas for integrating pronunciation into listening lessons

I didn't understand. Can I hear it again? When our learners ask us this in a listening lesson, we naturally play the recording again. In her book *Listening* (Oxford University Press, 1998) Goodith White points out that when we do this, we seem to 'hope that hearing it again will magically help the students to get the answer next time'. In fact, it might not be the vocabulary or the grammar in the recording that is causing the problems with comprehension. Instead, it is often the pronunciation.

1. Start by checking your lesson plan

A commonly used structure in listening lessons that many teachers feel comfortable with is as follows:

▶ Lead the students into the topic of the listening.

▶ Play the listening, answer some gist questions and check answers.

▶ Play it again, listen for more detail and check answers.

▶ Use the listening as the springboard for a speaking, reading or writing task.

However, this routine approach does not feature any pronunciation. So, think about where you could add a stage in your lesson plan which focuses on an aspect of pronunciation.

2. A pre-listening task

Before students listen, choose five content words (in other words, words which carry important meaning in the listening) which each have a different vowel sound; ideally, select words with phonemes you know the class has trouble distinguishing. In the lesson, write these five words on the board and either write the matching five phonemic symbols or five other words with the same sound. Ask students to match the words (or phonemes) by sound. Use this opportunity to pre-teach or clarify the meaning of these key words.

3. How does the speaker feel?

For a first listening task, focus on how the speaker feels. Emotions and mood affect intonation in particular. With an audio recording, show the students a photo of the speaker (or speakers) and ask them to predict their mood. Then ask them to listen to the recording, trying to get an idea of the feelings or attitude of the speaker. They shouldn't worry too much about understanding all the words. Afterwards, discuss how this person feels based on the sound of their intonation. With a video recording, you can turn the sound off first and ask students to watch the speakers only and predict their feelings. Then play the video again with sound on to compare their predictions.

4. Noticing accents and varieties of English

If you are using listenings with a wide variety of different voices from around the world, draw students' attention to the different accents and varieties of English. First, point out where the speaker comes from and talk about any particular pronunciation features of their voice. Over time, start to ask students if they can guess where the speaker comes from and say what it is about their pronunciation that tells them this.

5. Listening for key words

For the first listening, we often ask students to listen for the main gist or general meaning, so encourage students to focus on the main stressed words. For example, if the listening involves train announcements, students need to listen for stressed content words related to times and platforms. When listening to a weather report, they should listen for weather words and locations.

6. Identifying stressed words

Following on from Tip 3, draw students' attention to how certain key words are stressed. Turn the volume down a little and play the listening again. Ask the students to write down only the words they can hear. These will mainly be the words with most stress and the content words. Alternatively, let the students read the listening script and predict the stressed words by underlining them. Then get them to listen and compare what they hear with what they have predicted.

7. Listening more closely

When we play the listening a second or third time, we often set students the task of listening more closely for details. Quite often, this requires them to understand 'smaller words' like prepositions or articles. One way to develop this listening skill is to play only part of a listening; perhaps one or two sentences which are spoken at natural speed. Ask students to write down the exact words they hear and to compare with a partner. Then play it again until everyone thinks they have understood every word.

8. Identifying discourse markers

Discourse markers in listening texts are what make speech cohesive, organising what is being said. So, it is important that students can identify phrases and chunks such as *first of all, as I said earlier, I'll end by …*, etc. Noticeably, these kinds of phrases have fewer stressed words and therefore contain weak forms and features of connected speech. One way to help is to write any discourse markers from the listening on the board. Don't write them in the order in which they are spoken. Ask the students to listen again and number the markers in the order in which they are used. Another option is to play the discourse markers in isolation. Or again, the students could look at the listening script and predict and mark the weak forms or the linking between words, for example:

ə ə   ə ə
as a‿matter‿of‿fact

9. After listening

Another way to integrate pronunciation is to follow on from the listening stage with pronunciation based on a noticeable feature in the listening. For example, if the listening included a lot of question forms, you might focus on rising and falling intonation in questions. Alternatively, if the dialogue took place in a restaurant, you might concentrate on the **tʃ** sound in words like *chips, chicken, chops, chop suey*, etc.

10. Reflecting on your teaching

When we talk about pronunciation, we often think of it in terms of having students produce certain sounds, words and sentences. But pronunciation is also about understanding other people's speech, that is, it has a receptive element, in the same way that listening is a receptive skill. We need to allow plenty of time for students to listen to and identify features of pronunciation. Once students have listened for a rapid or highly connected pronunciation feature, teachers often feel they should also ask students to produce the same feature. However, this raises a question of whether it's desirable or necessary for students to try to produce the language using similar forms of pronunciation. Often, it isn't. Much will depend on the type of recording you are using and the context in which your students will need to speak, as well as listen.

Think back to some recent lessons you've taught recently. How often did you just concentrate on identifying the pronunciation features? How often did you go on to practise the phonological features? What might you change if you were to do the lessons again? Now, look at your upcoming lessons. Is there anything you need to change in your planning to solely focus on the identification of (a) pronunciation feature(s)? Is there a way you can add extra practice of this without asking your learners to produce the phonological feature? If you can, compare your ideas with a colleague's.

> "Songs can be an effective tool for practising pronunciation and facilitating learning of difficult sounds and words. Listening to songs helps students acquire the sounds and incorporate them into their own speech."
>
> **Magda Dygała, teacher, Poland**

10 ways to integrate pronunciation into reading lessons

When we think about teaching pronunciation, we often do so in the context of speaking and listening. But when you are planning a lesson which focuses on a reading text and reading skills, remember that there are ways to integrate pronunciation into these lessons, too.

1. Short texts or part of a text

For the purposes of pronunciation practice, choose a short text or one paragraph of a longer text that you have been using in class.

2. Listening and reading

After students have done the reading comprehension tasks with the text, set aside some time to read the text aloud. This could be you (the teacher) reading the text with students just listening and noticing the sounds of the words. Increasingly, many coursebook materials now offer a recorded audio version of the reading texts as well.

3. Circling words

Students read the text again and circle any words they are unsure how to say. It is highly likely most students will circle similar words, but you could begin by having students work in pairs, showing each other their words to see if their partner knows how to say them. Monitor their progress and make a list of the most commonly circled words. Write them on the board and say them aloud for students to repeat.

4. Noticing sounds

One useful noticing activity involves writing a phoneme on the board and asking students to read a text and to circle any instances of that phoneme. In this photo, the teacher has asked students to walk around the school and find examples of the schwa (ə).

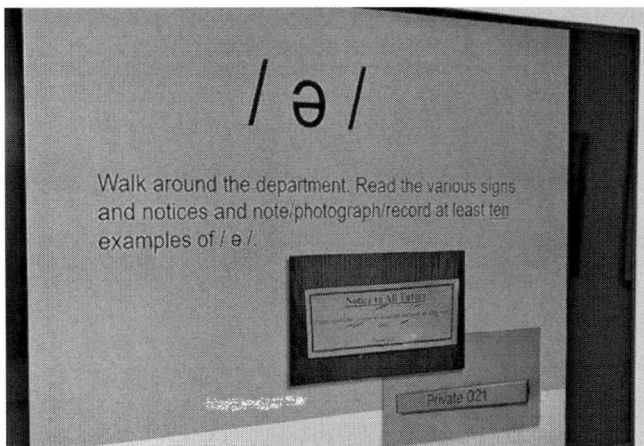

(Thanks to Jon Hird for sharing the image from his class.)

5. Words that rhyme

Before the class, study the text and look for any words that rhyme. Try to find four or five words that rhyme. Then give students the first word and tell them to look for any words which rhyme with it.

6. Words with the same sound

After students have read a text, you can give them the same text afterwards in the form of a gap-fill. It's a good way to recycle the text and help students remember certain words in the text. Another way to create the gap-fill is to remove words that have the same sound; for example, remove all the words with the sound **eə** (such as *pair* and *there*) and tell students to try to write missing words with that sound.

7. Word stress categories

Provide students with a blank table similar to the Word-stress table in Appendix 15.10 on page 158. Students categorise words from the text under the relevant word stress pattern. They don't need to categorise every word; you could ask them to categorise all the nouns or all the verbs or all the adjectives, depending on which type of words you want to focus on. Alternatively, students could categorise all the new words they have learnt from reading the text.

8. Dialogues and scenes

So far, all the ideas on this page have referred to the type of text you might have in a reading lesson. You can also use texts that are designed to be read aloud. These might include short TV sketches or scenes from a play. It could even be the audio script in the back of your coursebook. Students practise reading the dialogues aloud and you help with the pronunciation. When the students feel confident, they can perform the sketch to the class. This kind of task can act as a springboard into a writing task where students create their own sketches and dialogues.

9. Poems, rhymes, limericks and song lyrics

These text types are designed to be read aloud or listened to. They often have a rhythm, which is useful for focusing on sentence stress, and the final words in certain lines often rhyme. So, for example, if you were using the first four lines of the Beatles song *Yesterday*, you could remove the last two words in lines 2 and 3 (*away* and *stay*), and students would listen out for words that rhyme with *day*. With advanced students, you could just play the song and they would write down any words they hear with a similar sound to *day*.

10. Read aloud and record yourself

For follow-up homework, students practise reading a text aloud and record themselves on their phone. They can listen back and re-record until they feel happy with it. To check the pronunciation of unknown words in a text, encourage them to use a dictionary app that will play a recording of the word.

10 ways to help with sound and spelling

When a language decides to have only 26 letters but 44 different sounds, you know you've got problems! Learners must wonder at the craziness of a word like *thought*: where do you begin? They will find it particularly hard if their first language is a phonetic language (such as Japanese or Italian), where the tendency is to pronounce a word as it is written.

1. Begin with the positives

When helping students with sound and spelling in English, always draw attention to the positive news that most of the consonant letters in the English alphabet have only one sound, such as the **d** and **g** in *dog*.

2. Match the sounds

To introduce words with different spellings but the same vowel sounds, choose a selection of pairs similar to the ones below, which could be used with CEFR A1/A2 students. You could write them randomly around the board and get students to match them into pairs.

bed/said   rain/lane   bore/door   thought/port   sew/know   keep/eat

3. Digraphs

Raise students' awareness of **digraphs**. These are common combinations of letters producing certain sounds; for example, the spelling combination of *ph* often has the sound **f**. One simple way to explore digraphs is to choose a set of words which include the same spelling but with different sounds. Here is a set of words you could write on the board focusing on the digraph *ch*: *church, character, chart, chips, chaos, chat, choir, cheese*.

Students then categorise the initial sound of the word as either a **tʃ** or **k** sound.

(Answers: **tʃ** church, chart, chips, chat, cheese; **k** character, chaos, choir.)

4. Can you drop the 'e'?

This activity draws attention to the fact that when we add the letter 'e' to certain words, it changes the sound. Put up a selection of words ending in -e on the board such as these: *gate, hope, pine, leave, hate, gone, bite, love, note, mane, home, give, rode, cube*. Check students know how to say each one and explain the meaning if necessary. Then, in pairs, ask them to remove the letter 'e' at the end and decide:

1. Does this make a new word?

2. If so, how does the pronunciation change?

(Answers: *hop, pin, hat, bit, not, man, rod, cub*)

You could also point out to students that when you add 'e' to these types of words, the vowel letter sounds the same as when you say it in the alphabet; for example, the 'o' in *hope* sounds like the way we pronounce the letter *o* (**əʊ**).

Unit 33

5. Search engine exploration

Once students have become familiar with the idea that certain spelling patterns have different sounds, they can start to explore these by using any search engine such as Google. For example, if you want to focus on words with the letter combination 'ea', students could take a word like *beat* and try typing in the first part of the word 'bea'. They then see what other words are suggested. They'll discover other words like *beak, bear, beauty, bean* and can then try to find out how each word is pronounced and whether the 'ea' spelling ever changes. Next, they could try others with 'ea' spelling such as *hea-, mea-,* or *sea-*. They will discover words with similar and different pronunciation for 'ea' such as *hear/heart/head, meat/meal/mean, search/Sean/seal*.

6. Sound–spelling mazes

A sound–spelling maze is a fun way to look at problematic sound–spelling correspondences. Make copies of Appendix 33.6 on page 174. Students have to connect the two words in the shaded boxes by drawing a line that passes through other words that have the same sound. They can only go up, down, left or right, but not diagonally.

(Maze solutions: **u:** *through, flew, blue, group, loose, route, suit, flute, bruise, rude, food, do, Sue, threw;* **ɔ:** *nought, snore, law, door, lawn, poor, mourn, corn, thought, raw, sort, court*)

The additional blank version of the maze on page 174 is for you to devise your own. When choosing words to tempt students onto the wrong square, use words with the same spelling but different sounds (for instance, *flew* and *sew*) or words with similar or confusing sounds (such as *gate* and *get*).

(Thanks to Mark Hancock for inspiring this activity during a presentation.)

7. Delete the silent letter

So far, we've looked at spelling which might affect sounds, but another challenge for students is that English has silent letters in many (high-frequency) words. The next four tips suggest ideas for dealing with them. Begin by introducing the idea of silent letters. On the board, write a selection of words with silent letters and ask students to copy them down. Then read the words out. Students circle or delete the silent letter (or two silent letters in the case of *neighbour*). You could use this set of words or others that you have taught recently.

> climb   guitar   hour   island   knife   listen   night
> sandwich   Wednesday   walk   write   whole

(Answers: *clim(b), g(u)itar, (h)our, i(s)land, (k)nife, lis(t)en, ni(gh)t, san(d)wich, We(d)nesday, wa(l)k, (w)rite, (w)hole*)

8. Write in the missing letters

Write the words on the board but explain that one silent letter is missing in each word, like this: *clim   gitar   our   iland   nife   lisen*

Students can try saying the words aloud and then rewriting them correctly with the missing letter added back in, like this: *climb, guitar, hour, island, knife, listen.*

9. Connect the pair

Write a selection of words with silent letters around the board, making sure each word has the same silent letter as one other word. Here are 12 words you could use: *raspberry half every castle should knee high often   know though cupboard vegetable*
Students read them aloud and try to match the words with the same silent letter.

(Answers: *l = half/should k = knee/know t = castle/often gh = though/high p = raspberry/cupboard e = every/vegetable*)

10. Count the syllables

When spoken at natural speed, the letters become silent in certain words and they lose a whole syllable. For example, when written down, the word *interesting* appears to have four syllables. But normally, when spoken, the 'e' in the second syllable is silent, so it only has three syllables: *int(e)resting*. Write similar words on the board and have students write how many syllables they think the words have. For example, when said slowly, these words would have the number of syllable shown:

chocolate (3)	*different* (3)	*favourite* (3)
comfortable (4)	*family* (3)	*several* (3)

Then say the words at normal speed. Students decide which syllables (and letters) disappear. To help, you could say the word slowly first so that every syllable is spoken, and then repeat it at normal speed so a syllable is lost, like this:

choc(o)late (2)	*diff(e)rent* (2)	*fav(ou)rite* (2)
comf(or)table (3)	*fam(i)ly* (2)	*sev(e)ral* (2)

"Integrate pronunciation purposefully all the time with everything."

Adrian Underhill, trainer and author, UK

Unit 33

10 activities for spelling aloud

We introduce learners to the 26 letters of the English alphabet very early on. Beginner and elementary students usually start listening and repeating the letters in the first few weeks so that they can spell their names and ask for the spelling of new words. Nevertheless, spelling out words and recognising certain letters of the alphabet in spoken form remains a challenge for many learners, even once they have reached much higher levels of English. As such, it's always worth reviewing from time to time, and providing opportunities for practice. These ten activities begin with ideas for a basic introduction to spelling which will work at CEFR A1 or A2 levels; it then moves on to look at particular areas of challenge, and finally suggests more ideas which you can also use for review with higher levels.

1. Listen and repeat

Begin by writing the 26 letters on the board, pointing at each one and reading aloud. Students repeat them, as a class.

A B C D E F G H I J K L M N O P Q R S T U V W X Y Z

Listen carefully and make a mental note of the letters which your students find particularly difficult to pronounce. Then put students in pairs and let them practise.

2. Zed or Zee?

Pronunciation of the alphabet is fairly standard around the world. The only obvious difference is in the letter Z. The standard rule given is that British English speakers say 'Zed' **zed** and American English speakers say 'Zee' **zi:**. However, with the globalisation of English, it's probable that students will hear both. So, teach both pronunciations and let students choose which one they will use.

3. Remove a letter

Return to the letters on the board and delete a few of them, like this:

A B __ D E F ___ H I J ___ L M N O ___ Q R S T U ___ W X Y ___

Drill the letters again. This time, students try to remember the letters that are missing. Which letters you remove can be random: they could be every fourth letter, or they could be the ones they seemed most confident with in the activity described in Tip 1.

4. Group by vowel sound

We pronounce the letters of the alphabet using seven different vowel sounds, which can be grouped as shown in the table below. If students aren't familiar with the phoneme, you can add a word that uses the same vowel sound. In class, draw the table on the board with the vowel sounds (or words containing those vowel sounds) in the top row. Students try to categorise the letters into the columns as shown.

eɪ pay	iː me	aɪ my	e yes	əu no	uː you	ɑː are
A H J K	B C D E G P T V Z	I Y	F L M N S X Z	O	Q U W	R

ETpedia: Pronunciation © Pavilion Publishing and Media Ltd and its licensors 2022.

Unit 34

5. Challenging letters

In Tip 1 (on page 105), it was suggested that you make a mental note of the letters that students find difficult to pronounce. This is true for teaching at any level, and even learners with upper-intermediate and advanced English can struggle either to hear or produce particular letters. Certain letters will prove challenging for learners with different first languages. However, the vowels *A*, *I*, and *E* seem to be universally difficult for students to produce clearly, and, in particular, to distinguish between when listening. From time to time, write these letters on the board and set aside two or three minutes over a few lessons to review them and encourage students to practise saying them. Find words which contain more than one of them next to each other in the word and dictate them to the class, who write them down. For example, with the letters *A*, *I*, *E*, you could dictate words like *receive*, *wait*, *meat*, etc.

6. Silent spelling

This activity focuses students' attention on the shape of the mouth when spelling letters. Think of a famous person everyone in your class will know. Explain that you will spell this person's name, but your students will not hear it. Exaggerate the spelling of each letter in the name so the shape of your lips is very clear to students. Of course, the shape of the lips for some letters such as *C*, *D* and *E* won't change from being spread because the change is taking place inside the mouth. But because students are trying to guess the name of someone famous, they can note some possibilities and try to work it out from the clues given from the rest of the letters. It's a fun activity which draws attention to the importance of the lips in pronunciation. Once a student has guessed the answer, put them in pairs. Each student thinks of a famous person. In their pairs, they take turns to spell the name and write it down.

7. Developing a spelling strategy

Even for people with English as their first language, it's helpful to clarify a letter of the alphabet when spelling out a word (especially over the phone, for example). You might say a phrase like 'A, as in apple' or 'B for bus'. Sometimes people use an international spelling alphabet that is famously used by the police. Examples are 'Alpha' for *A*, and 'Bravo' for *B*, but it would be unhelpful to teach students this list. Instead, let them think of an obvious word they would choose for each letter and which they will feel confident using when needing to clarify the spelling of a word.

8. Guess the company

To add some authenticity to your spelling lessons, make use of the fact that many large companies often use acronyms for their names. Here are some examples, but you may also know of more from the students' own countries: CNN (news media), BMW (cars), YKK (zips), HSBC (banking), H&M (clothes), IBM (computers), BBC (TV), DHL (courier), LG (household appliances). You can use these to make up a quiz with two teams. Read out the company name. Students say its product, service or area of business. After you have done a few, students could work together and think of a few more to test their classmates.

9. Car number plates

Following on from Tip 8, another way to contextualise spelling authentically is to have students write down a few car number plate numbers (for instance, DXR 547 GE). Then write an example dialogue on the board like this:

Witness:	*I just saw a hit and run accident.*
Police officer:	*Did you see the plate number?*
Witness:	*Yes, it was DXR 547 GR.*
Police officer:	*Is that B for bear?*
Witness:	*No, D for dog.*

Students have a similar dialogue with a partner using some of the number plates they wrote down. Tell them to take turns to be the witness or the police officer who has to write the number down.

10. Secret messages

Make one copy of Appendix 34.10 on page 175 for each student. The page presents a secret code with instructions on how to decode it. Working individually, students prepare a message using the same code. Then, in pairs, they spell out their letters so that their partner can find the words and discover the message in the grid. The version provided will work with elementary and above, but you can also use the blank version on page 176, writing in words that are appropriate for your level, or words that you have taught recently and want to recycle.

"Pronunciation practice is important for comprehension as it supports and therefore motivates. Students need to hear words, phrases, and grammatical sentences so they can match sounds with spellings. They need to learn to hear the difference between can *and* can't *or* He liked dancing barefoot *and* He likes dancing barefoot; *they need to hear* what *enough, women, bus stop, etc. sound like to help their confidence in their own communicative abilities. "*

Fiona Mauchline, author and teacher trainer

Unit 34

10 steps for improving the delivery of a presentation

Many of your students will need to give presentations in English, either in the future or perhaps right away. Students who are studying English for their job might have to give presentations to clients and colleagues. Others who need English for academic study may have to give talks and lectures. Certain exams require students to give a short talk or presentation. As teachers, we also ask students to speak in front of the rest of the class; for example, presenting their opinions and ideas or talking about their personal interests or hobbies. Presentations are a challenging task for students but they can provide learners with a satisfying sense of achievement.

When improving the delivery of a presentation, it's important to include the use of gesture and visual aids, but the use of voice and clear intelligible pronunciation is key and that's the area that many of your students might be most concerned with. The following steps outline how to help your learners approach the preparation of a presentation. The main focus is on how to make sure that their pronunciation is not only clear and intelligible to their audience but also that it adds impact to their message.

1. Start with an extract

Begin by taking an extract of either a student's own presentation or an example of a presentation. You only need a short paragraph with three or four sentences. You could use the example below; it's useful because the speaker has to explain a technical process, so clear and slow speech is especially important:

Good morning everyone, and thanks for coming. Today, I'd like to give a short presentation about a scientific process called photosynthesis. It's the process in which the leaves of plants take the energy from sunlight and, as a result, the plants turn carbon dioxide into oxygen. Let's begin by looking at this slide, which shows the process in more detail.

Give one copy of the extract to each student and make sure there is plenty of space between the sentences for students to mark the extract. Alternatively, make copies of Appendix 35.1 on page 177 and hand out them out. Initially, ask students to read the extract while you read it aloud as if you are giving the presentation. Then answer any questions about the vocabulary in the text before moving onto the next stage (in Tip 2).

2. Listen and mark the pauses

Explain to students that when we speak in English, we add pauses between sentences or slight pauses in parts of a sentence. This is most noticeable when we speak more slowly and formally. Adding pauses when presenting makes the language easier to deliver for the speaker and clearer for the audience. Read the extract in Tip 1 aloud to the students. Make sure you pause clearly where longer pauses (//) are indicated between sentences and where shorter pauses (/) are indicated mid-sentence. Ask students to listen and mark the pauses in the extract where they think they hear them. You will need to read it two or three times before showing the answers.

Good morning everyone / and thanks for coming // Today / I'd like to give a short presentation / about a scientific process called / photosynthesis // It's the process / in which the leaves of plants / take the energy from sunlight / and / as a result / the plants / turn carbon dioxide / into oxygen // Let's begin by looking at this slide / which shows the process in more detail //

3. Elicit guidelines

Based on the answers in Tip 2 (on page 108), ask students what they think the rules or guidelines might be when deciding when to pause. Elicit the following:

You should pause:

- *at the end of sentences*
- *when there is a comma*
- *sometimes before a conjunction such as and*
- *either side of a conjunction to stress there is more to come*
- *either side of key words, such as the title of the talk*
- *to break down very long sentences.*

Emphasise the point that some are rules and others are guidelines which will depend on the type of presentation.

4. Read aloud in pairs

Put students into pairs and let them practise reading the presentation extract aloud to each other, trying to insert pauses in the correct places. Monitor the students as they read and give initial feedback or help with the pronunciation of any individual words before moving onto the next stage (in Tip 5).

5. Stress a word

Explain that in every group or chunk of words between two pauses, we usually stress one word in particular and sometimes two. Demonstrate with the first phrase written on the board and say it, stressing the underlined word: / *Good morning everyone.* / Then read the extract aloud again. Students underline the stressed words they hear you use:

Good morning everyone / and thanks for coming // Today / I'd like to give a short presentation / about a scientific process called / photosynthesis // It's the process / in which the leaves of plants / take the energy from sunlight / and / as a result / the plants / turn carbon dioxide / into oxygen // Let's begin by looking at this slide / which shows the process in more detail //

6. Changing the stress

With more advanced groups, you could also point out that it's possible to change the stressed word to slightly alter the meaning or emphasis. For example, you would generally say / *Good morning everyone* / but you might say / *Good morning everyone* / if for some reason you wanted to stress the fact that you are welcoming all the people in the room, not just a few. Or you could stress the word *short* to let people know you won't take a long time, for instance / *Today, I'd like to give short presentation*/

7. Intonation

With very advanced levels, you might analyse the intonation patterns in the extract in Tip 5 (page 109), but for most classes, point out that the intonation will tend to rise in a word like / *Today* / in sentence 2 because there is more to follow, whereas it will fall in the word / *photosynthesis*, which is at the end of the sentence. It will be more effective to read the text aloud in two ways: first, read it in a robotic monotonous tone with no intonation; then read it again with engaging and natural intonation. Students will easily recognise the difference and try to apply this.

8. Apply the techniques

Having shown students the difference that using pauses, stress and intonation will make to their delivery, ask them to apply the same techniques to their own script (or an extract from it). Point out that they shouldn't read a script in a presentation word for word, but that practising this way will help improve their delivery. They can practise at home or with partner in class.

9. Make recordings

Encourage students to record themselves reading the script before applying pauses. They record themselves again after they have practised pauses, and then again after working on stress and intonation. In this way, students build up a tangible portfolio of recordings that demonstrate their improvement, which can be very motivating. On specialist presentation skills courses, some trainers ask their trainees to send them a recording. They then give feedback on it before the student tries again.

10. Time to present!

Set aside time for students to give their presentations to the whole class. Note that classroom presentations can be time-consuming, so spread them out over a series of lessons. If you teach online, students could deliver their presentations on-screen or by recording their voices with their slides and sharing it.

"There is no 'best' English and no 'best' pronunciation. Everything depends on your ability to adjust your speech to the person(s) you are speaking to. Experts call this accommodation. If you cannot accommodate, you will not be successful in international communication."

Evan Frendo, Language training consultant, Berlin, Germany

Unit 35

10 ideas for integrating correction

Deciding when and if to correct a student error is probably one of the most complex skills a teacher needs to develop. And with pronunciation, it requires the ability to think on your feet and decide how to respond.

1. Stop and think before you correct

When you hear a student make what might be considered a pronunciation mistake, ask yourself the following series of internal questions, and then act upon the answers.

- ▶ Is it really a **mistake** or just a difference in accent or choice of English pronunciation?
- ▶ Would it be acceptable in some varieties of English?
- ▶ Does it affect intelligibility?
- ▶ Is it just a slip? (A **slip** is a mistake that the student wouldn't normally make and so it doesn't need attention.)
- ▶ If it is a mistake, has it been taught before? If not, maybe wait.
- ▶ If it is a mistake, why is the student having that difficulty?
- ▶ Is it something that can helpfully be corrected on the spot, or will it need more time in class?
- ▶ Is it only a problem for this learner, or is it something that affects the whole class?

2. Contrast two ways of saying it

Correcting students on the spot works best when the error is one that a student will recognise and have the ability to change. For example, if a student says 'sill' but you think that they may mean 'seal', you can repeat their pronunciation followed by the alternative, like this: 'Sill or seal?' In this way, the student hears both words and notices the difference between them. Then they choose the word they mean and try to say it again.

3. Hand gesture

Using the example given in Tip 2, you can hold the palms of your hands close together when they say 'sill' to indicate the vowel sound is short and then hold them further apart when they say 'seal', to indicate a longer sound. As students get used to this, you can even say a word like 'sill' and coax them to produce the longer vowel sound by moving the palms apart but not saying anything. Students self-correct because you are prompting them with your gesture.

4. Humming

If a student says a word with the stress in the wrong place, you can hum the word back to them without saying it. For example:

Student:	I'm going to give a preSENtation.
Teacher:	mm-mm-MM-mm
Student:	presenTAtion. I'm going to give a presenTAtion.

5. Fingers

Fingers are an excellent tool for quick correction. Hold up the fingers on one hand to represent the number of syllables in a word or the number of words in a sentence. Then hold two together to show two words which are contracted. One situation where you can use this technique is when, often at lower levels, students struggle to contract two words and would rather say *I am a student* instead of *I'm a student*. You might argue that this doesn't affect intelligibility, but as students become more proficient, they normally want you to point this out. One way to coax them towards contracting the sounds is to count out their sentence on four fingers (*I. am. a. student.*) and then hold the first and second fingers together to represent *I'm a student*. Once students have become used to this technique, you can do it without speaking – the action alone will coax students towards saying *I'm*.

6. Your mouth

If the problem is with a phoneme sound and it can be solved by noticing the shape of the mouth or the position of the tongue and lips, clearly model the sound so the student can see the shape and movement of your mouth. With online teaching this can work particularly well because you can move your mouth closer to your webcam.

7. Point at an articulators of speech diagram

If the problem is occurring because of place and articulation in the mouth which you can't show with the shape of your mouth, point at an **articulators of speech diagram** (see Appendix 9 on page 151), and show which ones are in use.

8. Write on the board

If students are familiar with the phonemic symbols, it's helpful for them to see a visual representation of what they said and what you want them to say. For example, if they are making a mistake like *I like <u>at</u>* instead of *I like <u>art</u>*, you can draw one like this **æ** and another like this **ɑ:**, and point out the difference. If you do write on the board, be very clear about which is the error and which is the correct version. Avoid leaving the error written incorrectly on the board in case other students copy it down, thinking it's correct.

9. Peer feedback

Sometimes, when students are discussing something together in pairs or groups, you might overhear an error. Before you intervene, wait: the other student might either peer-correct or – because the error has caused a misunderstanding – realise the problem and resolve it as part of the conversation.

10. Recording

Students record a short piece of speech they are working on. They play it back and listen out for any errors. Then they record themselves again as many times as they wish until they are satisfied with the recording. Next, they send the recording to you for feedback. You can either give your feedback later in class or record it for them to listen to later. See Unit 42, pages 127–128, for ten ideas on recording students' pronunciation.

10 tips for teaching pronunciation to young learners

This unit focuses on tips and activities to increase your effectiveness in the young learner classroom. While these tips do not exclude older learners, they are an important part of the fun element in the young learner classroom.

You can find lots more ideas for using songs, chants, rhymes, tongue twisters and stories in *ETpedia Young Learners* by Vanessa Reis Esteves (2016, Pavilion Publishing and Media).

1. Make it visible

Making pronunciation visible to young learners activates different areas of awareness that can aid in recall of sounds and pronunciation. Show the word in both its written form and, if it's an obvious verb, adjective or noun, as a flashcard image to ensure that meaning is at the forefront of pronunciation focus. Use gestures to show the intonation going up or down, and exaggerated facial movements to show how the muscles in your mouth move. Drawing intonation patterns above sentences is another way of making pronunciation visible.

2. Make it colourful

Colour adds to the visible component of pronunciation. This can be done in a number of different ways:

▶ showing stressed and unstressed syllables in different colours

▶ writing silent letters in a different colour

▶ showing the stressed words in a sentence in different colours

▶ showing alternating syllables in different colours (especially longer words)

▶ writing the schwa sound (the vowel, not the symbol) in a different colour from other letters across a range of words

3. Moving in seats

Younger learners like to move, so think about ways to include movement in a pronunciation activity. If students can't leave their chairs, they can at least stand up in their places. Use this to focus on the word stress and the number of syllables. For example, the word 'banana' contains three syllables, and the main stress is on the middle syllable. Students say the word and stand up out of their seats on the middle syllable.

4. Free movement

If you can clear the chairs and tables to create a large open space (or even go outside into the school playground), students can move freely. Put four separate words, such as *pit*, *pot*, *pat*, *pet*, each on a large piece of paper at the four corners of the classroom. (The four suggested words have been chosen to contrast their different vowel sounds.) Say one of the words. Students move to the corner where the word they have heard is displayed. After you have done this a few times, say other words which have a similar vowel sound, such as *sit*, *sat*, *not*, *let*, *lot*, *bit*, *bet*, *bat*. Again, students move to the corresponding corner. As students become confident, put them in groups. Student take turns shouting one of the words with the rest of the group running to the word they hear.

Unit 37

5. Tongue twisters

Finding tongue twisters online is easy; they are a great way to help young learners with individual sounds, word stress, and sentence stress. They can also highlight homophones and homonyms, and make students aware of similar-sounding words with different meanings – take this one for instance: *If two witches watch watches, then which witch watches which watch?* Where possible, make sure the students actually understand the tongue twister, so they understand why saying it wrong means it doesn't make sense. It also helps with coming up with 'answers' to tongue twisters. For example: *The witch with the black watch watches the black watch, and the witch with the red watch watches the red watch.*

6. Songs

As Vanessa Reis Esteves says, a good song 'can stick in our ears and memories for a whole day. This means that when children learn [it], they will be picking up and practising language without realising it' (*ETpedia Young Learners*, 2016:56). If you have a recording of the song, play it loudly at first, and encourage learners to sing along with it. As the class becomes familiar with the song, reduce the volume of the recording until only the students are left singing along.

7. Chants

As with catchy songs, chants will also stay with students and provide natural practice of English. Often, a chant features a particular phoneme at the end of a sentence, such as the **eɪ** sound in 'Rain, rain, go away, come again another day'. Because of their nature, chants also develop awareness of rhythm and sentence stress. As you teach a chant, it's often useful to have students clap the beat at the same time. Once they become familiar with it, add variety by speeding it up, so students have to try and sing faster and faster without making a mistake.

8. Rhymes

Children tend to learn rhymes almost unconsciously but at the same time, saying rhymes can make them aware of and practise different sounds. For example, this one focuses on the **æ** sound:

There was a cat

which ate a rat

And then it sat

On a big black mat

9. Stories

Stories are great for pronunciation practice because of their easily comprehensible nature; moreover, traditional children's stories often have a repetitive structure that students can produce on their own. Think, for example, of the story of 'The Three Little Pigs', in which a wolf tries to blow their three houses away. The wolf says… 'I'll huff, and I'll puff, and I'll blow your house down!' This is an effective way to focus on the **ʌ** sound in the word 'huff' and 'puff' without making it a very formal lesson.

10. Reading aloud

Reading aloud from simple story books gives young learners the opportunity to produce extended stretches of language with support. It also allows the teacher to notice, correct and address pronunciation issues, and to ensure that this pronunciation focus is done within a clear and comprehensible context.

"I take photos of members of the class making the different sounds. Being young learners, this is always great fun as they never turn down the opportunity to pose! The photos then become a visual guide displayed around the classroom which I can use to teach or correct, and a constant reminder that pronunciation is physical."

Olivia Price-Bates, academic director, Italy, learninglessonsfromtefl.com

Unit 37

Section 5:
Online teaching and technology

With so many lessons taking place online, it's important to consider how we can approach pronunciation teaching and learning in this environment.

The first part of this section begins with tips and considerations for live online teaching with video-conferencing tools and how you approach it. We also look at how technology also offers us new opportunities and potential ways of making our pronunciation teaching more engaging and effective.

Then we look more broadly at the range of online technology available for developing pronunciation, before, during and after a lesson, with pointers to useful websites which foster learner autonomy.

10 tips for teaching pronunciation with a video-conferencing platform

For teaching live lessons online, many teachers use video-conferencing platforms such as Zoom or Microsoft Teams. After teaching pronunciation in a face-to-face classroom, moving your lessons online can feel challenging. Here are some tips on how to adapt your teaching for an online lesson and how to make the most of your video-conferencing platform.

1. Rename your profile

Most platforms show your profile name when you log on. The platform usually allows you to rename yourself. If yours does, introduce the idea of 'a phoneme for the lesson', and have students choose a new name for themselves which uses that phoneme; for example, if you choose **k**, students could rename themselves Karl, Kathy, Kate, Kaitlyn, Kyle, etc. You could tell students what it will be the lesson before, and they could research their new name for homework.

2. The webcam

The webcam is a useful tool for the lesson. When teaching pronunciation, you can get your mouth close to it and show students the shape of the mouth when you produce certain phonemes. You can also use it to see what shapes your students are producing.

3. Sound on, sound off

You can model pronunciation with the sound on, but you can also switch the sound off and mouth a word so students can watch your mouth shape without the sound. Drilling the whole class can be challenging because of different internet speeds, so one option is to tell students to keep their sound off and just practise on their own after they have heard you. This is similar to the idea behind a mumble drill (see Unit 8, pages 31–33).

4. Screenshare

The screenshare option in a platform allows you to present slides, documents or pages from a book, or to share a virtual whiteboard. One advantage it has over the face-to-face lesson is that students can easily annotate the board as well. In the example below, the teacher has written the phoneme in the middle and asked students to write any words they can think of that start with that sound.

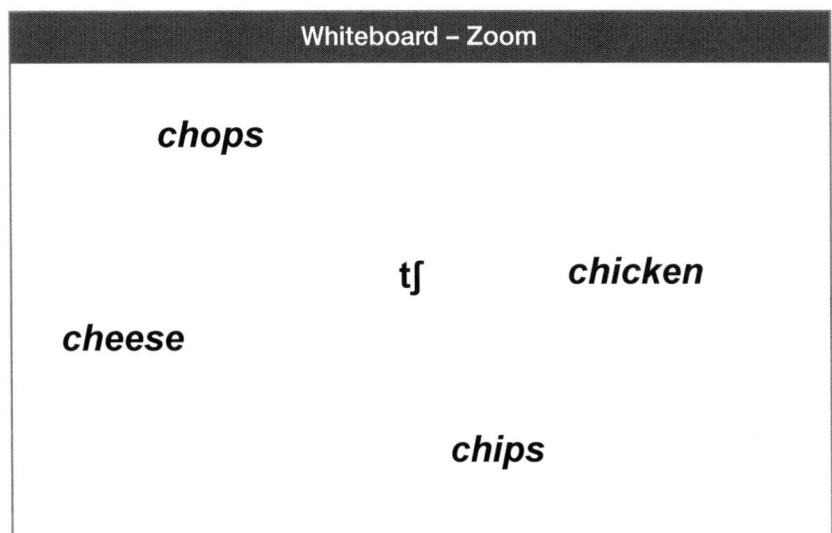

5. Chat

One way to use the chat box to quickly illustrate pronunciation features is to use underlining between words to show linking, and capital letters to show word and sentence stress. It's especially effective for on-the-spot error correction.

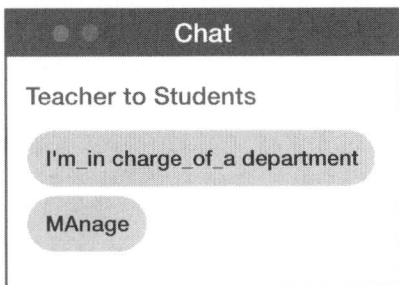

Chat

Teacher to Students

I'm_in charge_of_a department

MAnage

6. Reactions

Most platforms have a reaction function with various symbols, such as a thumbs-up and some emojis. They are a useful way to gauge what students are hearing. For example, you could read out minimal pairs, and students would have to use the reactions to indicate what they hear. So, for the sounds **ʊ** and **u:** you could read out minimal pairs like *pull/pool* and *full/fool*. Students show the palm emoji if they think they heard a word with the shorter vowel sound **ʊ** or thumbs-up if they heard the longer vowel sound **u:**. They show the face if they aren't sure and want to hear it again.

7. Poll functions

A poll function can be a quick way to find out what the whole class is hearing. For example, you could focus on emphatic stress by giving students a choice of four sentences, as shown below.

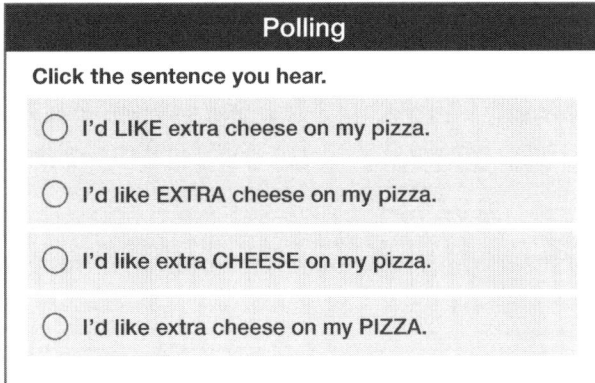

Polling

Click the sentence you hear.

○ I'd LIKE extra cheese on my pizza.

○ I'd like EXTRA cheese on my pizza.

○ I'd like extra CHEESE on my pizza.

○ I'd like extra cheese on my PIZZA.

Read one sentence aloud, stressing the word in capital letters. Students click the sentence they think they hear. The advantage of this activity is that students who choose the wrong sentence are not exposed because the poll is anonymous. Afterwards, you can talk about how stressing these words in capitals affects the meaning of the sentence in four ways.

8. Breakout rooms

The drawback of doing pronunciation practice in breakout rooms is that it is harder to monitor. However, the advantage of sending students to a breakout room in small groups to practise pronunciation is that it gives them a safe space to practise and make mistakes. So, if you want everyone to practise reading a text aloud or preparing a presentation in pairs, breakout rooms provide this option. You can also 'drop in' to individual breakout rooms and deal with any problems.

9. Recordings

Platforms such as Zoom also offer a record function, so students have an easy way to record a stretch of speech or a role-play conversation. They can then share the recordings with you for feedback on their pronunciation. If your classes are too big for that, encourage students to listen to their own recordings. They often realise what they need to work on just by listening to themselves. (See Unit 42, pages 127–128 for more ideas on using recordings.)

10. Adapting activities for online lessons

List some of your favourite pronunciation activities which you often use in your face-to-face classroom. Consider how you might use the same activity online and which video-conference functions you could use.

"In a live online lesson you can use various types of silent dictation. This is where you have your video on, but your audio is muted. For instance, have a series of sentences that represent clear actions. You 'dictate' the sentences and do the actions (e.g. I woke up. I yawned. I checked my phone ...) and students write them down. Dictations like this allow you to focus later on the sounds and particularly the articulation you when making them."

Lindsay Clandfield and Jill Hadfield, authors of *Live Online Teaching* (2021, Pavilion Publishing and Media)

10 benefits of online pronunciation teaching

When working online, especially in synchronous live lessons, it's worth being aware of the pros and cons so you are well prepared.

1. Close-up in the webcam

Unlike in a classroom, students can see up close how the teacher's mouth moves when pronouncing certain sounds or words. The presence of the camera or webcam mean that the teacher can position their face close to the camera to highlight and model how words are produced and exactly how the mouth moves. It is also possible to isolate certain parts of the word or certain sounds, and highlight these with the camera.

2. Equality

Following on from Tip 1, all students can see the teacher equally well through the webcam, unlike in a face-to-face classroom, where the teacher might be less visible to students sitting in the back of the room. In other words, it's easier to model effectively for the entire class at once.

3. Easier to see students

If students have their cameras turned on, the teacher can closely observe their mouth movements when they produce words and sounds, and this makes it much easier to diagnose issues. In a face-to-face classroom, the teacher would have to move around the room and get close to students, potentially making them feel uncomfortable. With cameras on, the teacher can see each student clearly, and can ask them to move nearer to the camera.

4. Recording the lesson

The lesson, or parts of the lesson, can be recorded so that students can listen and watch the pronunciation again in their own time. Note that recording the entire lesson produces a very large file, but that might not be necessary. If you record only the part of the lesson where the focus is on pronunciation, you will have a much smaller file that can be shared and managed more easily.

5. On mute

One way to build confidence in an online lesson is to have students switch their microphones off when you first introduce a word and drill it. You speak with your microphone on, and then they practise without anyone hearing them (and without them hearing anyone else except the teacher). This means they can generate some level of comfort with the new words or phrases before having to say them in front of other students.

6. Attention to mouth movement

Teachers looking at students producing words with their microphones off can focus more on how the students' mouths and facial muscles are moving. This can be turned into an activity to practise pronunciation. One student says a word with their microphone muted, and the other students have to guess what the word is. This can also be done with short phrases. The benefit of doing it online is that unlike the classroom activity, where students try to say the word without producing any sound, they can actually say the word out loud, but with the microphone muted.

Unit 39

7. Seeing their own mouth movements

With cameras on, students can pay attention to their own mouth movements and facial expressions. This helps them notice how they are forming and producing sounds, something that is impossible in a classroom (unless students carry mirrors with them or look into their phones during the class).

8. Recording and sharing

With pronunciation activities like minimal pair activities, students can record themselves and send the recording to a classmate. This means that when the teacher checks for misunderstandings or inaccurate pronunciation, there is actually a record of what was said. This helps with diagnosing and highlighting pronunciation problems much more effectively.

9. Self-recordings

When students are introduced to new language in the classroom, they usually have to wait until the class has ended before they can record anything they want to listen back to later. In an online class, the student can momentarily mute themselves, and record the new word onto their phone. This can be done directly after the word has been modelled by the teacher. Then they have an immediate and accurate record of the pronunciation of the word.

10. Online video review

As a homework task, encourage students to search for online videos about pronunciation. Suggest ways in which they might do this by looking on a search engine and typing, for instance, 'How do I make the **j** sound in English?' A variety of videos will be suggested so tell them to choose three. Then they watch them and report back to the class which of the three videos they preferred the most and give reasons why.

"I get students to practise by filming themselves speaking and then they upload the videos on a private YouTube channel for self-assessment and peer assessment."

Mardiana Idris, teacher, Malaysia

Unit 39

10 reasons for using technology

This unit looks at how using technology can enhance your pronunciation teaching and the pronunciation of your students, both productively and receptively.

1. Analysing pronunciation

Teachers are generally very good at identifying errors and issues in the classroom, but with everything else that we have to manage, it's easy to miss or overlook pronunciation issues that might be systemic. Using technology to make recordings or, for example, voice-to-text technology, means you can listen to and analyse your students' pronunciation in more detail after the lesson.

2. More opportunities to practise and connect outside the classroom

For many students, especially those who live in a country where English is not spoken as a first language, the classroom is often the only place where they get to practise English. Technology allows for spoken communication to happen outside the classroom via online platforms like Zoom or Skype, and even via certain social media platforms like WhatsApp. In addition, students can send voice recordings to you or other students via text.

3. Learner autonomy

Technology has the potential to let students take charge of their learning; they can choose what they want to focus on and how and when to do so. It personalises the learning process and puts the learner in control of what they want to work on beyond the classroom. For example, they could choose YouTube and TikTok videos that they are interested in and focus on accents from specific parts of the world (see Tip 7 on page 124).

4. Self-monitoring skills

Recordings allow learners to listen to themselves and to focus on how they pronounce certain words. It helps them to notice and correct their own problems. This is a critical skill as it creates awareness of weaknesses and puts the individual in control of what they are trying to improve.

5. Preparation

Technology allows learners who struggle to speak in front of others to practise speaking using recordings. Recordings allow learners to review what they want to say, preview vocabulary and phrases, listen to them, and practise until they are comfortable. They can then be ready to use them in the classroom.

6. Reducing avoidance

In productive activities, learners often produce what they know and avoid structures and words they are uncertain of, perhaps because they are afraid to mispronounce them. Using technology outside the classroom allows learners time to practise items they are unsure of until they are ready to use them in the classroom. This also ties in with autonomy (see Tip 3 above) as the learner can choose to practise something specific they want to use and not avoid it when speaking to others.

7. Increasing exposure to different accents

With all the videos and recordings that are freely available online, learners can now easily be exposed to a number of different accents and pronunciation models. This is important as learners are likely to encounter a variety of different speakers and accents, and it is difficult for teachers to expose them to such a wide variety within the limitations of the classroom.

8. More focused error correction and feedback

Recordings allow teachers to listen to specific parts of learners' speech without the distraction of being busy in the classroom. This means that they can give more focused error correction. The teacher can, for example, record and send back to the student the accurate form of a word or a phrase, and provide much better feedback than if they had to listen to ten students all speaking at once during a productive task in the classroom.

9. Tangible sense of progress

Technology lets students make a recording of their voice, then work on improving their pronunciation and record the same piece of speech again. Students can then compare the two recordings of their voice to establish how much they have improved.

10. What technology do you use?

Think about the technology available to you for use in your teaching and, indeed, what you use socially to communicate and listen/watch content. Then consider how it could be used to develop your learners' pronunciation. Are there any ways it might help that you couldn't normally do in a face-to-face lesson?

"Dictionary apps can help students practise the pronunciation of new or difficult words. For homework, ask student to list 3–5 words they find difficult to pronounce, and to download a free English-English dictionary app. Students play the audio recording of the word in the app, and listen and repeat until they feel more confident with the pronunciation. In class, ask the students to orally share a few of their chosen words – in sentences. Setting this homework task regularly may help students improve their pronunciation over time."

Nicky Hockly, author of *ETpedia Technology* (2017, Pavilion Publishing and Media)

Unit 40

10 ways of incorporating technology

In this unit we look at ways of incorporating technology into pronunciation teaching. It suggests some general uses of technology, and also refers to some specific sites that are especially helpful when it comes to working on pronunciation.

1. Speaking on audio software

For extended speaking tasks, like storytelling or picture descriptions, students can record their answers on applications like Adobe Express or Audacity. This allows the teacher to listen to them individually, and allows peers to listen to their classmates. It also means that learners can listen to themselves and identify areas they would like to work on.

Another way of using a recording app is for peer discussions, for example, the type required in collaborative tasks in Cambridge Main Suite exams. Learners can listen back and assess how well they manage such skills as turn-taking and working towards an outcome. The teacher can listen and highlight areas of pronunciation to work on.

2. Using headsets/earphones/ear buds

In a classroom, if learners have headsets, earphones or ear buds, they can listen to each other's recordings and provide feedback. If you set such a listening task, ensure that learners are given specific instructions as to what to listen for. Another use for in-class headsets, earphones or ear buds is for learners to listen to recordings or parts of recordings more than once. Teachers often don't have enough time in class to replay every part of the recording that students are struggling with, but if learners have the option to download the recording onto their phone, they can easily replay part of a listening.

3. Authenticity

The website Youglish.com allows users to find authentic uses of phrases on YouTube. For example, if there is a particular phrase or set of words that the teacher wants to focus on, they can enter the phrase into Youglish.com and find authentic examples of the phrase in use. They can then use these clips in the classroom to highlight pronunciation, collocations, and how collocations lead to connected speech. Students can also be encouraged to use Youglish.com at home to find authentic examples of language they want to learn or practise.

4. Subtitles and scripts

Subtitles and scripts with videos (such as with TED Talks) provide a rich source of language and plenty of examples of natural speech in which students can notice features of pronunciation. One effective activity that uses subtitles involves choosing part of the video and playing it with no subtitles. Students listen and write what they hear, as they would in a dictation. Then they watch again with subtitles and compare what they wrote with what is written on the screen.

5. Videos of mouth movement

Video platforms like YouTube host a wide selection of pronunciation videos showing how the mouth moves when it produces individual sounds and words. Some even come with explanations of what the mouth is doing, so they are useful for students to watch in class or on their own at home.

Unit 41

6. Slow down speech

When playing audio in a class or using videos on YouTube or other platforms, it is often possible to slow down the audio to make it easier for students to notice the pronunciation of individual words. This is particularly useful for highlighting connected speech and word boundaries. You can then go back to normal settings and encourage students to notice how these word boundaries are realised or connected when spoken at speed.

7. Lyrics training

Lyricstraining.com is a website where you can select a song for students to listen to, and then give them a gap-fill task that is automatically generated. It is particularly motivating for students who like pop music as they can choose a song they enjoy and then learn all the lyrics. It often throws up a number of surprises because what you hear is often not what the singer is actually singing.

8. Flipgrid

Flipgrid is a video tool that allows a teacher to select a topic or a task and have students make and post their own videos in response to the topic or the task. Students can re-record their videos as many times as they wish until they are happy with the result. This means they can check and re-check their own pronunciation, or ask others, including their teacher, to comment, before the video goes live.

9. Recorded text messaging

If students are using a text-messaging application like LINE or WhatsApp, they can send a recorded voice message. Not only is it a much quicker way of sending longer messages, but it is also a great way for students to listen to their own and each other's pronunciation and provide the teacher with material from which to identify pronunciation issues.

10. Teacher recordings

Teachers can record new language and send it to students through email or on messaging applications. This allows the teacher to select the specific language they want students to focus on, but it also allows learners to leave the classroom with a record of the language that was covered in the classroom. This is particularly helpful if there was any emergent language that is not on the coursebook audio.

10 questions about recording students' voices

Maybe one of the most under-used techniques for helping students to improve their pronunciation is having them record their own voices. This unit thoroughly explores its value.

1. Why do teachers avoid recording students?

Logistically, recording students can be complicated. If you have a large class, it's impractical to record everyone and listen to every recording. Also, recording in the classroom can be difficult if everyone is speaking at the same time. Another obstacle is that many people don't like hearing their own voice or watching themselves on video, so your students might be resistant to it. Finally, once you have the recording, what do you do with it? Let's look at reasons why we record and what can be done in tips 2–10.

2. How can recording be effective?

Having a recorded sample of students talking is invaluable for teachers. It helps them to avoid making assumptions about the kind of difficulties that a group of students will have (for example, because of their nationality and first language); instead, it allows them to focus on the individual learner and the type of support they need. Training students to record themselves is also a way of developing learner autonomy. They can listen back and pick out their own issues and work on them.

3. What type of things do students record?

Students can record a list of recently learned vocabulary, which they share with you for checking. They might also record a short lecture or talk so that they can get feedback from you. (See Unit 35 on pages 108–110 on improving delivery of a presentation.) Remember, also, that a recording might involve two or three students discussing something or doing a role play, and it could be in the form of a video or an audio file.

4. How can I record my students' voices?

If your students have a phone, it probably contains a record function. If not, they can download one of the many voice-recording apps. The website Vocaroo is one the simplest tools for recording and sharing a voice. Note that if you are recording students in class, or you need a better-quality recording, you can try connecting an external microphone to your laptop or video camera to record. For online teaching, try using a tool like Zoom, which also has an easy-to-use recording function.

5. How can I persuade reluctant students to record their voices?

If you anticipate resistance from students, make a few things clear from the outset: anything they record will be private and listened to only by you or by some of their classmates for peer-review. Start off in a small way: pairs of students could record a dialogue they have written and then listen back to themselves. Slowly build students' familiarity with the idea of making recordings; for example, some students feel more relaxed making a selfie-video of themselves talking. If this is the case, have them make video recordings with the intention of focusing solely on pronunciation. One final tip is to provide a task which has a different aim, but that generates a recording as a result. For instance, the app Fotobabble allows you to upload a photo of your choice and then record your own description of the photo. It's fun for students to share photos they have taken, and to tell others about it on Fotobabble. By doing so, they also provide the teacher with an invaluable stretch of speech.

ETpedia: Pronunciation © Pavilion Publishing and Media Ltd and its licensors 2022.

Unit 42

6. How can students share the recordings with me?

The easiest way for students to share their recordings is for them to make an audio file and email it to you or share the link to an app that records and will create a link.

7. Should students record the same thing more than once?

Definitely. For example, if a student is preparing a short talk, they can record it once, then send it to you or another student, who listens and gives feedback. Then they record it again and try to make improvements. A student can record the same text a few times, and by the end they will have a portfolio of recordings which demonstrates tangible evidence of improvement.

8. Do I ask them to record their voice in class or for homework?

It depends on your situation, but it's often more practical for a student to make the recording at home or away from other external noise. If you are teaching online, using a tool like Zoom, students can work together in breakout rooms and record their conversation there.

9. How can I teach students to analyse their own recordings?

Guide students by giving them a checklist or feedback form to follow. This might be a form that you give to all your students to use, or it could be a personalised set of criteria that you give to a student based on what you already know about their pronunciation. For instance, a teacher has given this simple checklist to a student who is recording his personal information as if he's leaving it on a voicemail:

▶ Did you sound friendly when you introduced yourself?

▶ Did you pronounce the J and G in your name differently? (Remember that J rhymes with *may* and G rhymes with *me*.)

▶ Did you say your telephone number in **chunks**? (For example, 0204 / 326 / 8756)

10. How can I record my feedback on students' pronunciation?

The quickest way to add your feedback is to record your comments straight after their recording. Listen to the recording, make notes, and then record your feedback. You can pick out an aspect of their pronunciation and say it correctly or you can suggest ways to improve. If you have a written version of the text, record yourself saying it as a model so the student can listen and try again.

10 websites and tools to incorporate in pronunciation teaching

This unit recommends websites, apps and online resources that either provide authentic models of speech or allow learners to use technology to review and practise pronunciation outside the classroom. Where the site has a URL, we have just provided the name so that you can find it in a search engine (as web addresses often change).

1. Speech Accent Archive

There are hundreds of different accents to listen to on this site. It is particularly useful for students to hear speakers with their own first language speak English, or to hear English speakers with a specific first language if they frequently interact with that group.

2. The International Dialects of English Archive

This site is a rich resource of people with different accents reading a specific paragraph and then talking about a topic. Scripts are also supplied so learners can compare what they think they have heard with what was actually said.

3. BBC Learning English

This BBC site offers a variety of resources including a section on the schwa, connected speech and spelling. It is easy to navigate, and while it may appear limited in what it offers, it still remains a good site for students and teachers to access for ideas and tips on pronunciation.

4. Sounds of speech

This app has been created by the University of Iowa. It offers a very detailed resource that would be especially useful on more academic English courses. It offers diagrams of the mouth and explanations of the manner and place of articulation. There are also video clips of people producing each of the sounds. Overall, it's a very complete reference – something that is likely to appeal to high-level adult learners and, potentially, trainee teachers.

5. Google Search

If you want students to learn how to check their own pronunciation (before asking you) show them that if you go to Google Search and type in the word like this, 'Pronounce + [the word]', Google shows you the word broken down into syllables and a mouth saying the word. Students can also click the 'Practice' button (when you select American pronunciation), record themselves saying the word, and get basic feedback.

6. Saylists

Initially set up to help children with speech therapy, Saylists features songs focusing on specific sounds (mainly problematic consonant sounds) in English. The large selection of songs means there should be a song in each category for everyone. Saylists focuses on sounds in initial, mid, and final position in words.

7. TED Talks on Lingorank

TED talks offer a vast bank of authentic speech featuring a range of accents and nationalities. Lingorank arranges these talks by CEFR level. This allows students to notice and practise features of pronunciation while they follow the content of the talk.

ETpedia: Pronunciation © Pavilion Publishing and Media Ltd and its licensors 2022.

Unit 43

8. Sounds right

This simple app is from the British Council helps learners with the sounds of English; they can use it as an alternative to a dictionary. It's also a useful app for teachers who are training and need to become familiar with the phonemic symbols.

9. Voice dictation software

If you type 'Voice dictation' into any app store, you'll find a selection of apps which are designed to listen to your voice and transcribe the words you are saying. There is also an inbuilt recording function in the Microsoft Office suite and in smart phones and devices. Whichever way you access it, the software is a useful way for students to record themselves and notice how their speech is transcribed by it. When the software transcribes their words incorrectly, they can try to record the text again and see if they can alter their pronunciation accordingly.

10. Editable audio software

Programs like Audacity and WavePad allow learners and teachers to make recordings but also edit them. This can be useful for teachers who wish to cut out parts of a listening text so that students can listen to a specific pronunciation feature. Learners can use it to record themselves and edit parts by recording over them or adding them into another recording.

"Websites such as elllo (elllo.org) are a good resource for short clips of spoken English delivered by speakers of different nationalities."

Edmund Dudley, author of *ETpedia Teenagers* (2018, Pavilion Publishing and Media)

Unit 43

Section 6: Materials writing and professional development

As you become more confident as a pronunciation teacher, you might be involved in selecting course materials or coursebooks. So, the first unit in this section suggests ten questions to ask yourself about the coursebook or materials you plan on using.

If you find that published course materials lack the focus on pronunciation you require, you might consider writing your own supplementary pronunciation exercises and lessons for you and your colleagues to use in class. To help you with this, Unit 45 gives advice on how to write some basic activity and task types for pronunciation. Given the nature of pronunciation, you might also need to create recordings to use with written activities and tasks and to help you with this, you'll find Unit 46 explains how to prepare and make your own recordings. In addition, if you are looking to design more creative, interactive activities for pronunciation lessons then Unit 47 will help you with that.

The remaining units focus on further development and how to manage your progress as a pronunciation teacher. The final unit provides a list of recommended English teaching books about pronunciation for you to read after this one.

10 pronunciation in a coursebook questions to consider

If you are in the position of selecting a coursebook (including sets of course materials or an online platform), part of your analysis should include questions about the status of pronunciation in the material. Here are ten questions you could ask yourself about the books you are choosing from. They are also useful questions to ask yourself if you are designing your own materials. You might not always be able to answer 'yes' to all of them but try to select materials that fulfil most of these criteria.

1. Is there at least one item (and preferably more) of pronunciation in every unit?

2. Does the book include featured sections on pronunciation?

3. Is there a good balance between presentation and practice?

4. Is pronunciation integrated into the grammar and vocabulary sections?

5. Is there a balance of focus on segmental and suprasegmental pronunciation?

6. Is there a balance between productive and receptive pronunciation practice?

7. Do the recordings include non-native as well as native speakers, with a range of accents from around the world?

8. Does the book include authentic recordings?

9. Do the pronunciation activities look fun and motivating to do?

10. Does the material also include self-study pronunciation practice for students to do on their own?

10 types of activities for writing pronunciation materials

Among the many published materials that exist, both on the page and online, you can find activities written for teachers to use with their classes and for students to do on their own. However, most of the material available is for grammar and vocabulary; there is far less for pronunciation. As such, if you want to present and practise a particular aspect of pronunciation that your learners find difficult, you might decide to write your own material.

The next two units suggest a variety of activity and task types that you can easily write and adapt for your own classroom context. This first unit looks at ten of the most basic – but useful – types of activities and tasks you can write for pronunciation, with the focus on presenting the pronunciation for the first time. You could also use them if you have to write short tests to check students' progress.

1. Listen and notice

When writing activities for pronunciation practice, we often think students should 'do' something, such as repeat what they hear or write something. In fact, when you are presenting a new aspect of pronunciation, you can simply play the audio and let students listen without the pressure of having to speak as well. If you want to guide them to notice specific elements of the pronunciation, you can design your task like this example from a lesson worksheet on the topic of sport.

Listen to these words. What do you notice about the stressed syllable?

1. compete   2. competitive   3. competitor   4. competition

Answer: The second syllable is stressed in 1–3. It changes in 4.

---

2. Listen and repeat

If your aim is only for students to listen for certain pronunciation features, a 'listen and notice' task, as described in Tip 1, is useful. However, many students will also want to try and produce the target pronunciation, in which case, 'Listen and repeat' activities work in class or for self-study. The format works for all pronunciation features; students can listen to and repeat individual sounds, word stress, connected speech and intonation. Try not to make what they are repeating too long; any utterance longer than, say, five or six words becomes too difficult to repeat. The sample activity below comes from a lesson practising the language for making polite requests; it includes phrases that are probably about as long as you should reasonably go.

Listen and repeat these sentences with the same intonation.

1. Could you help me?

2. Would you mind giving me a hand?

2. Do you mind helping me?

---

3. Listen and circle

To get students to identify what they hear, give them two easily confused items and ask them to circle the one they hear in the audio. This type of task works well with minimal pairs. For example:

Listen and (circle) the word you hear in each sentence.

1. hit   heat   2. dip   deep   3. lip   leap

Audio: 1. Please turn down the heat. 2. Be careful. The water's very deep. 3. Ow! I bit my lip!
Answers: 1. heat 2. deep 3. lip

---

4. Listen and match

'Listen and match' activities work well when you want students to match words with the same sound but different spellings. It might look like this:

Listen and match the words with the same vowel sound.

1. sad	a) lied
2. said	b) owed
3. side	c) bad
4. sewed	d) he'd
5. seed	e) bed

Answers: 1 c) 2 e) 3 a) 4 b) 5 d)

---

5. Listen and choose

Giving students three or more choices is a common way to test pronunciation; it also encourages them to think about what might confuse them when listening to everyday speech. Have them listen to a word and choose the word they hear from three options. For example, if the word was *heart*, they could choose between the following three words:

1. *hat*
2. *heart*
3. *height*

6. Listen and mark

We often 'mark' pronunciation features in some way; for example, we might mark the stressed syllable in a word, the intonation pattern on a phrase, or the linking in connected speech, as shown in the example below. Note that the way in which you ask students to mark a pronunciation feature in an exercise should be consistent with the way you normally mark features on the board and in class.

Unit 45

> **Listen and add a linking line:‿between words in these phrases.**
>
> 1. Can I ask a question?
>
> 2. Did our package arrive?
>
> 3. What time is Mike arriving?
>
> Answers: 1. Can‿I‿ask‿a question? 2. Did‿our package‿arrive?
> 3. What time‿is Mike‿arriving?

7. Listen and categorise

Grouping or categorising activities is a common way to help students see connections and similarities between features. For example, they might listen to words and group them according to a shared vowel sound, a stressed syllable or similar intonation patterns. In this example, students categorise the pairs of words by the linking or intrusive sound that can occur in everyday speech.

> **Listen for the sounds w, j or r between the pairs of words and write them in the table.**
>
> 1. go in   2. the apple   3. her aunt   4. he answers   5. do it   6. tear off
>
> | w | j | r |
> |---|---|---|
> | 1. go in | | |
>
> Answers: **w** 1, 5 **j** 2, 4 **r** 3,6

8. Listen and correct

Design this task so students have a list of correct and incorrect items. They listen and decide which are incorrect and then try to correct them. The example here shows how a task like this can be designed for word stress. Students listen to the words and decide if the stress pattern is correct.

> **Listen to these words. What do you notice about the stressed syllable?**
>
> 1. compete   2. competitive   3. competitor   4. competition
>
> Audio: 1. Germany 2. American 3. Switzerland 4. England 5. Portugal
> Answers: 1. incorrect Ooo 2. Correct 3. Incorrect Ooo 4. Incorrect Oo 5. Correct.

Unit 45

9. Listen and complete

Activities which get students focusing on listening for pronunciation in extended speech are good for developing their ability to deal with connected speech. Give students part of the sentence but miss out one or more words. They listen for the missing words and write them in the gap. In this example, the writer has removed any words which will be affected by features of connected speech.

Listen and write in the missing words.

1. Would _____ like a cup _____ tea?

2. Could _____ have an _____?

3. Do _____ mind giving me _____ lift?

Audio/Answers: 1. Would you like a cup of tea? 2. Could I have an apple? 3. Do you mind giving me a lift?

---

10. Listen and write (dictation)

Another simple task that takes students beyond individual sounds and words involves playing sentences or a complete text and asking students to write what they hear. This form of dictation is a useful way to reuse recordings from past exercises. If you have already used an exercise like the one shown in Tip 6 on page 135, reuse it, asking students to listen and write the phrases out in full.

"A well-written piece of pronunciation material makes something complex seem simple. I like this metaphor: 'The better the diver, the smaller the splash'."

Mark Hancock, author of the PronPack series (2022, Hancock McDonald ELT)

Unit 45

10 tips on scripting and recording pronunciation materials

The previous unit described how to write pronunciation activities and tasks. In addition to writing them, you might also need to write scripts and record them (either on audio or video). This unit provides advice on how to approach this.

1. Basic recording equipment

It has never been easier to record audio. Most smartphones and devices have functionality that is capable of making a good-quality recording that you can play in class. Alternatively, you can buy a reasonably priced handheld recording device to record your voice.

2. Improving the recording quality

If you want to guarantee really high-quality recordings of audio scripts, use an external microphone which can be held close to the speaker. A small clip-on microphone is good for recording people when you're out and about; a larger microphone – the type that is used for making podcasts – offers extra functionality to improve the quality of the recording.

3. Audio recording software

Your laptop or tablet might come with some basic recording software already installed. This will probably make a serviceable recording, assuming you make sure the room has good acoustics and there isn't external noise. However, if you want software which offers additional features, such as editing tracks and reducing external noise, you can use an open-source audio app like Audacity, which is free to use.

4. Writing 'listen and repeat' audio scripts

If you plan on writing your own audio scripts for pronunciation materials, think carefully about the aim of the scripts. For example, if the script is going to be for 'listen and repeat' tasks, where the teacher plays the audio recording and students listen and then repeat a word or phrase, then you need to build in clear pauses between each word or phrase. And the pause needs to be of an appropriate length for the students to speak. In the audio script below, which has been written for a studio recording, notice how the full stop between the two words indicates a short pause and then a longer pause between each item is also indicated in square brackets. (Note that the script was written for a task to contrast the minimal pair of **b** and **p**.)

Voice 1:	Ball. Paul.
	[3 second pause]
Voice 2:	Bet. Pet.
	[3 second pause]
Voice 1:	Bin. Pin.
	[3 second pause]
Voice 2:	Back. Pack.

Unit 46

5. Writing 'listen and tick' audio scripts

Following on from Tip 4, if you are writing a script in which students listen and tick what they hear, you will still need a pause between each word or phrase so students have time to read and tick. Here's an example of a 'listen and tick' exercise and the script you might write to go with it:

Listen to the word. Do you hear b or p?

1. **b**   **p**
2. **b**   **p**
3. **b**   **p**
4. **b**   **p**

Audio script

Voice 1:	Ball.
	[3 second pause]
Voice 2:	Pet.
	[3 second pause]
Voice 1:	Pin.
	[3 second pause]
Voice 2:	Back.

6. Writing extended dialogues

The scripts in Tips 4 and 5 were examples of what might be written for pronunciation tasks looking at single phonemes, words or short phrases. If you want to write more authentic-sounding scripts which, for example, demonstrate features of connected speech, you can write these like a normal script for a play or a film. If you are going to record it with actors, you will need to decide how fast the lines are to be delivered. For example, with materials for students at CEFR A2/B1 level, the pace of delivery is often slightly slower than in everyday speech. On the other hand, you might want the students to be exposed to authentic-sounding pronunciation, in which case you can let the actors deliver it at normal speed.

7. Actors and accents

If you are going to record the voices of actors (including friends and colleagues), try to include a range of voices and accents to reflect the varieties of English around the world. The exception to this would be if you are preparing your students to work with speakers in a particular country, in which case try to include accents from that country in your recordings.

8. Authentic speech

Another way of sourcing authentic English (if you live in a place where English is spoken) is to ask people for an interview, for example in the street or around your language school, and record them. Of course, it's harder to control what people say and to produce a recording that targets a particular pronunciation point. However, if you choose your interview questions carefully, you can probably get useable responses. For example, if you ask a question like *What sports do you like?*, you will probably get answers using the ŋ sound, as in the words *playing*, *doing*, *going*, *watching*, etc. On the other hand, when people speak freely about any topic, you will also get interesting examples of connected speech, which can be used effectively with higher-level learners.

9. Video recordings

If you plan to make video recordings (instead of just audio), your main consideration will be what students might gain from seeing the speaker as well as listening to them. For example, if you are teaching attitudinal intonation (see Units 23–24, pages 71–76) it is important to see the speaker's expression; after all, our expressions and emotions are closely linked to our intonation. Another reason for making a video recording is that it allows students to see the speaker's mouth. For example, if the audio script in Tip 4 (on page 137) was made with video, you could have a close-up of the speaker's lips.

10. The format of the recording

The way in which your recordings are to be delivered for use will affect how you record them. Most teachers want recordings as an audio file that they can play in their classroom from a laptop, tablet or phone. If the recording is to be part of a self-study online course, you will need to check whether the format of your audio or video file will work on the learning platform; even if the file type is compatible, sometimes it is too large or loads too slowly. In many cases, you can change the file type, but doing this is time-consuming, and it's better to check before you start recording.

"Limericks are my favourite type of script to write for pronunciation practice. They're great for rhyme, repetition and humour."

Sue Kay, author and co-founder of ELTteacher2Writer

Unit 46

10 types of interactive activities for pronunciation materials

In this unit, the ideas for writing your own materials are less controlled and more game-like, and they get students working together. You often find these types of activities in teacher resource materials, in the back of teacher's books or on websites that accompany course books. This unit outlines the ten main types, with reference to photocopiable pages which you can adapt for your own purposes.

1. Dominoes

In dominoes, students have about six or seven dominoes each and take turns to match each one in some way, creating a long line. The winner is the student who successfully gets rid of all their dominoes first. Dominoes work well for practising matching things like rhyming words and word stress – see Appendix 15.7 on page 156 and the dominoes blank template on page 157.

2. Snap!

Deal a set of cards equally between two or more players. Each player plays a card at the same time and if two cards match in some way, the winning player shouts 'Snap!' first and takes all the cards on the table. In effect, it's a type of matching activity. You can remove the competitive element and just have students try to match all the pairs in a set of cards. It works well for matching individual sounds, word stress and sentence stress (see Appendix 15.4 on page 153).

3. Pelmanism

The game of Pelmanism works in a similar way to 'Snap!' You need a set of cards with pairs of cards that match in some way. In groups, students shuffle all the cards and turn them face down on the table. The first student turns two over. If they don't match, the student turns them face down again and the next student tries. If the two cards match, the student takes them and has another go. At first, students won't get many matching pairs, but over time, they start to memorise where certain cards are, and they find it easier to turn over matching pairs. When all the cards have been taken, the winner is the student with the most pairs of cards. See Appendix 19.7 on page 163 for an example of a Pelmanism game, and page 164 for a blank pairs template.

4. Board game

With a board game you need a series of squares with a 'Start' square and a 'Finish' square. Each player has a counter which they place on 'Start'. Then they roll a die or toss a coin (heads = move 1 square, tails = move 2 squares). Each square will have a task. For example, you could write a phoneme on each square, so that when students land on it, they have to say a word with that sound. Alternatively, students might have to say a word with the same stress pattern. You can adapt the blank basic board game in Appendix 47.4 on page 178 for your own purposes.

5. Bingo

In Bingo, the teacher calls out words or sounds and students tick each one off on a card they are holding. Each card is slightly different, so students will be ticking off different words and sounds from each other. When a student has ticked off a complete line, or all the items on their card, they shout 'Bingo!' It's a good activity for listening and noticing. See Appendix 19.2 on page 160 for bingo cards, and a set of blank bingo cards.

6. Crosswords

If you have taught students the phonemic symbols, you can create a crossword in which students have to write the phonemic symbols. The clues are the actual words; students have to transcribe them into the crossword. Alternatively, you could design it the other way round so that students read the phonemic symbols as clues and complete the crossword with actual words. For another interactive crossword that can be used as a pairwork activity, see Appendix 26.8 on page 170.

7. Mazes

Mazes are time-consuming to make but intriguing to use. Look at the sound-spelling mazes in Appendix 33.6 on page 174 as examples – there's also a blank maze template you can use. You will need to create a grid of squares and design it so that students have to find their way through the maze by matching words with certain phonemes. When creating mazes, begin by establishing the correct route, and then add the distractors in the other squares.

8. Noughts and crosses

The idea behind a noughts and crosses game is that you draw a three-by-three grid on the board and divide the class into two teams. One team is noughts (0) and one team is crosses (X). The aim is to get three noughts or three crosses horizontally, vertically or diagonally. In the activity in Unit 22.9 (page 166), students have to say phrasal verbs with linking in a sentence in order to write a nought or a cross. But the game can be adapted so you have, for example, nine different phonemes or nine different word stress patterns and the teams have to give you a word with the phoneme or the correct word stress (see Appendix 22.9 on page 166 for a photocopiable version and a blank template).

9. Hidden treasure

Look at the hidden treasure game in Appendix 47.9 on page 179. Students think of words and write them into the grid. The words could be based on a lexical set you have recently taught, such as 'food' or 'sport'. Then, in pairs, they take turns to call out a square by saying, for example, 'A5' or 'F1'. If the other player has a word on that square, they have to say the letter and state how many letters there are in the word. The player can keep guessing the other letters when they 'hit' a word. If they guess correctly, they have another turn. If not, the other player has a turn. Play continues until a player has discovered all the words on the other player's grid. It's a good activity for practising spelling out words.

10. Find a partner

For a game-like activity to get students out of their seats and moving around, make a set of similar-sounding words (see Appendix 19.7 on page 163) and give one card to each student. The students move around the room saying their word and searching for someone else who (in this version of the game) has a word with the same stress pattern. They then move around in their pairs looking for other students (either a single student or another pair) who have words with the same stress.

10 pronunciation questions to consider

The subject of pronunciation teaching causes some of the most heated debates in the world of English language teaching. The more you teach pronunciation, the more questions and views you may have. Here are ten of the questions that are often debated in teachers' rooms, on blogs and at language teaching conferences.

1. Which English is being used as a pronunciation model?

If you use a coursebook published by a British publisher, it is likely to offer a British English pronunciation as the standard model. However, as many teachers born in the UK soon discover, it's a rather misrepresentative standard. For example, in RP, the standard pronunciation of the word *bath* is **bɑːθ**, but for many teachers (often from the northern parts of Britain) the pronunciation is **bæθ**. Similarly, books published in the US often include a standard pronunciation called 'General American', which doesn't necessarily represent the accents of every American teacher.

2. What other varieties of English can I teach?

There are many other countries with English as their first language, for example, Australia, South Africa, Ireland, and so on. We can also refer to other **global Englishes**, including Singaporean English, Nigerian English or Indian English. In addition, there are many more speakers of English who use it as their second language and whose accents are specific to their region. So, the question of what English pronunciation we teach is far more complex than it first appears. For more on this topic, see Sandra Lee McKay's *Teaching English as an International Language – Rethinking goals and approaches* (2002, Oxford University Press).

3. Should I teach English as a lingua franca?

One response to the issue of what standard to follow has been the idea of an **English as a lingua franca (ELF)**. In 2000, *The Phonology of English as a Lingua Franca* by Jennifer Jenkins was published (Oxford University Press). In it, she argues that we need a new approach to teaching pronunciation in which intelligibility is the priority for English learners, rather than an attempt to imitate native speakers of a so-called 'Standard English' such as British English. Instead, we should talk about ELF or English as lingua franca, in which English is a means of communication used globally and not 'owned' by one or two nations. After all, your students are far more likely to communicate with other people for whom English is not their first language so concentrating on intelligibility rather than perfection seems a sensible way forward.

4. What is intelligibility?

If pronunciation teaching is about helping learners to be intelligible, we need to establish what we mean by **intelligibility**. In *The Phonology of English* (2002, ELB Publishing), Ray Parker and Tim Graham point out that teaching students a standard English isn't much use if the person listening to you isn't familiar with or 'tolerant' of that standard. The implication, then, is that we need to identify who our students will be communicating with. If they are going to visit, study in or work in the UK, they need to be familiar with listening to and approximating a British English accent. But if they are going to communicate from their office in Germany with someone in Brazil using English as the means of communication, the ability to reproduce British English pronunciation is not necessarily going to make them more intelligible.

5. Whose accent do I teach?

Many teachers are concerned by this question because they feel their accent is not the same as the main accent demonstrated in the coursebook or that it doesn't match a 'standard'. The answer is that you teach with your own accent. As for your students, the aim is to make them intelligible; if their accent does not affect their intelligibility, they might want to keep that accent and many teachers would argue that they should do so.

6. Is pronunciation primarily receptive or productive?

The expectation of many classrooms remains that if we can hear it, we should be able to produce it. However, this depends on your students' needs. For example, a student may be able to distinguish weak forms, yet be unable to produce them in rapid speech. So lesson aims could divide pronunciation into features that students should be able to understand and those that they need to be able to produce.

7. Can pronunciation be categorised according to CEFR levels?

We readily put students' grammar and vocabulary abilities into levels, with terms such as **elementary**, **intermediate** and **advanced**. Rightly or wrongly, we all have a view on when to teach the present simple and when to introduce conditionals. Similarly, we can now identify the CEFR level of an item of vocabulary using a dictionary and decide when is an appropriate time to teach it. But as Patsko and Simpson point out in their book *How to Write Pronunciation Activities*, 'pronunciation features are all potentially present from day one'. Because of this, pronunciation tends to be either integrated into the teaching of other aspects of language or isolated to match the needs of the learner (for example, if a learner makes a mistake with a phoneme and it needs correcting). Patsko and Simpson add that this is 'no bad thing, as it perhaps reflects more realistically the way we tend to acquire language' (2019:51).

8. Is it always teachable and learnable?

What might be easy to teach might not be so easy to learn. For example, we might find rules for a particular intonation pattern and tell our students that intonation always goes up or down under certain circumstances. However, few students are ever likely to achieve this subtlety in their own English, and our classroom time might be better spent on more achievable goals.

9. Do my teaching materials contain enough pronunciation practice?

As a teacher you may be allowed to choose your own coursebook or teaching. Or you have reached the stage where you are responsible for selecting materials for your language school. However, you may be given a set coursebook to work from. Whichever way your course material is selected, it is worth reviewing how the pronunciation work is treated and what kind of practice it provides your learners (if any) – especially if pronunciation already forms a key part of what you teach. Use the questions in Unit 44 on page 132 to help you analyse your current coursebook or materials, and then to help you select/create new materials if appropriate and if you feel that you need to encourage more pronunciation in lessons.

Unit 48

10. What do your colleagues think?

As you can see, there are not always hard-and-fast answers to the questions listed in this unit. Answers might be affected by your teaching context, the needs of your learners and your own philosophy on teaching pronunciation. If possible, discuss some of the questions with your teaching colleagues and find out what they think; maybe together you can develop a school policy on your approach to pronunciation.

"Ask students if they find it easy or difficult to tell where native speakers of English are from based on their English pronunication. What about non-native speakers of English? Do they have any favourite varieties of English pronunciation? Discussions of this kind help to steer students away from pre-conceived ideas about what 'proper' pronunciation sounds like, and enable you to celebrate diversity."

Edmund Dudley, author of *ETpedia Teenagers* (2018, Pavilion Publishing and Media)

10 tips for continuing professional development

Here is some final guidance to help you with your ongoing development towards becoming an effective pronunciation teacher, including tips on how contribute to other teachers' further development.

1. Experiment

Not all the activities and tips in this book will work in your teaching context. Experiment with activities and then reflect on what worked or didn't work and why. Doing this will allow you to adapt it to your context, giving you a much deeper insight into your learners' needs and pronunciation teaching in general. Start with one activity, reflect and adapt. Then do the same with a second, and a third, until you have a trusted repertoire of activities to go to.

2. Keep a pronunciation diary

Once you start experimenting with activities, and reflecting on how well they work, or attending online webinars and face-to-face events, it becomes very difficult to keep track of all the great ideas. One way of keeping track of the ideas and your reflections is to keep a pronunciation diary. This will make it easier to find pronunciation-specific notes and ideas than if you just had a general teaching diary. Make sure to include details of the class(es) you've used the materials with, what's worked well and what needs improving, with a note about what to adjust or try for next time.

3. Create

Learning to write and create your own materials (as outlined in Units 46–48, pages 137–144) is a great way to develop your skills. It means that you design materials that are specific to the needs of your learners, and you can also have fun being inventive and creating game-like materials.

4. Share

The activities we design for our classes are aimed predominantly at our own students, and they often fit with our own approach to teaching. Sharing activities allows other teachers to experiment with your ideas and to provide valuable feedback that could be used to improve them. Their feedback might also help you when you come to teach a different level or in a different context.

5. Become an IATEFL PronSIG member

Consider becoming an IATEFL member and joining the IATEFL Pronunciation Special Interest Group (**PronSIG**), which is the IATEFL Special Interest Group (SIG) that focuses specifically on pronunciation teaching – you get one free SIG entry with your membership. The group provides a platform for teachers to exchange ideas and activities, discuss methodology and best practice, and to connect teachers who are interested in pronunciation across the globe. They have many free events, such as webinars and social media; registered members also receive additional benefits such as the SIG publication called the *Speakout! Journal*.

Unit 49

6. Write an article for *Modern English Teacher* on pronunciation

Once you have received feedback from peers, sharing more widely allows for even more feedback; it also supports learners and teachers in other contexts. One way of sharing your activities and insights into pronunciation teaching more widely is to publish an article with *Modern English Teacher* (*MET*, www.modernenglishteacher.com). You can contribute even a small activity for the feature 'It works in practice'. The readership is global and it provides a platform for feedback and sharing that far exceeds your own teachers' room or local context. Find out more by visiting www.modernenglishteacher.com/write-for-us.

7. Blogging

Another way of sharing your activities or insights into pronunciation teaching is to start a blog that chronicles your pronunciation teaching journey. Many bloggers develop quite large followings, with many teachers visiting the blog regularly to read what they have to say. If you decide to try this, remember that you will need to write a post on a regular basis. Alternatively, you could write a 'guest' blog post to appear on someone else's blog. Either way, the research that goes into a blog post is a great way to develop your skills.

8. Present a webinar

Webinars are a great way to reach colleagues in many different countries; you have the chance to present your ideas to a wide range of teachers, and they can share their ideas with you, too. Teachers who are in a different time zone, or who are unavailable at the scheduled time, can view a recording of your webinar later. As such, your contribution to the field of pronunciation (and to your own development) will be visible, and will hopefully inspire others.

9. Present at a conference or workshop

You might find presenting at a conference stressful at first (and even many experienced presenters say the feeling of stress never entirely goes away), but interacting face-to-face with an audience, having discussions with like-minded colleagues and making connections are all invaluable experiences. One way of starting off is to present at one of the IATEFL PronSIG local/online events or even leading a teacher development session in your school.

10. Train others

Training other teachers is perhaps the most valuable area of further development because when you train others, you have to ensure that have a strong understanding of the subject. For example, when are a trainee on a course like the Trinity Diploma TESOL, you make sure you know enough so you can pass the phonology interview. When you train others, you make sure you know enough so *they* can pass. The increased level of research and reflection that comes from training others to improve their pronunciation teaching is bound to be beneficial for your development.

10 more recommended books to read and refer to

Here are ten more resources that teachers can refer to related to pronunciation teaching. These books cover the basics of pronunciation teaching, more in-depth analysis of key issues, and a look at English as a lingua franca and intelligibility. Note that this is by no means an extensive list.

1. *How to Teach Pronunciation* **by Gerard Kelly (Pearson, 2000)**

   As part of the Pearson 'How to teach …' series, this is an easy read covering all the basic areas of pronunciation, individual sounds, and segmental features of pronunciation. It also has lots of useful activities that are simple for both novice and experienced teachers.

2. *Sound Foundations* **by Adrian Underhill (Macmillan Education, 2005)**

   Adrian Underhill is one of the best-known pronunciation experts in English language teaching, and his book appears on the reading lists for both the Trinity Diploma TESOL and Cambridge DELTA. It is packed with lots of information and ideas for teaching pronunciation. You can watch Adrian Underhill's accompanying videos on YouTube.

3. *Learner English*, **edited by Michael Swan and Bernard Smith (Cambridge University Press, 2001)**

   This book sets out learner challenges based on their first language. It covers a whole range of aspects of language, but it is an extremely useful book for teachers who need an insight into the pronunciation difficulties of specific groups of learners. It is useful for teachers of both monolingual and multilingual English classes.

4. *Phonology for Listening* **by Richard Cauldwell (Speech in Action, 2013)**

   Primarily focusing on listening, this book looks at how to help learners decode the sounds of speech by looking at phonology. It is useful for both novice and experienced teachers, and provides a clear theoretical rationale in the introduction and first two chapters, followed by lots of examples and practical classroom applications.

5. *The Book of Pronunciation* **by Jonathan Marks and Tim Bowen (Delta Publishing, 2017)**

   As part of the Delta Publishing Teacher Development series, this book begins with an introduction to pronunciation, going over all the important areas of pronunciation. This is followed by a large section describing a wide variety of activities. The last part focuses on additional areas to consider when teaching pronunciation, and encourages reflection.

6. *English Phonetics and Phonology* **by Peter Roach (Cambridge University Press, 2001)**

   This book provides a detailed course on phonetics and phonology. It covers topics in depth, and concludes with a comparison between Received Pronunciation and other common English accents. This should be a must-read for candidates doing a Trinity Diploma, a Cambridge DELTA or a Masters in TESOL.

Unit 50

7. *Teaching the Pronunciation of English as a Lingua Franca* **by Robin Walker (Oxford University Press, 2010)**

This book makes the case for teaching **English as a lingua franca (ELF)** pronunciation in a clear and digestible manner, and addresses some concerns about teaching ELF pronunciation. There are also chapters on the implications this could have on teaching, and some ideas for classroom implementation.

8. *The Phonology of English as an International Language* **by Jennifer Jenkins (Oxford University Press, 2000)**

Based on data of miscommunication between non-native speakers of English, and the fact that non-native speaker interactions in English outnumber native-speaker interactions, this book proposes and discusses in depth the Lingua Franca Core (LFC) and its effect on intelligibility between non-native speakers. It argues that a 'core' set of pronunciation features affect intelligibility globally, and that teachers need to focus on this 'core' with their students rather than 'non-core' items. It's an excellent book by one of the leading figures of the pronunciation of English as lingua franca.

9. *Intelligibility, Oral Communication and the Teaching of Pronunciation* **by John Levis (Cambridge University Press, 2018)**

This book forms a bridge between research and classroom practice. It is divided into four parts, focusing on the theoretical framework, word-based errors, discourse-based errors and implications for research and teaching. With a strong focus on intelligibility, this book is a great resource for helping students become more intelligible and decoding the speech of other speakers.

10. *50 Tips for Teaching Pronunciation* **by Mark Hancock (Cambridge University Press, 2020)**

Neatly divided into three sections, this book covers pronunciation goals and models, what to teach, and how to teach it. It offers a good mix of theory and practice from one of ELT's most prolific authors on the topic of pronunciation.

Unit 50

Appendix

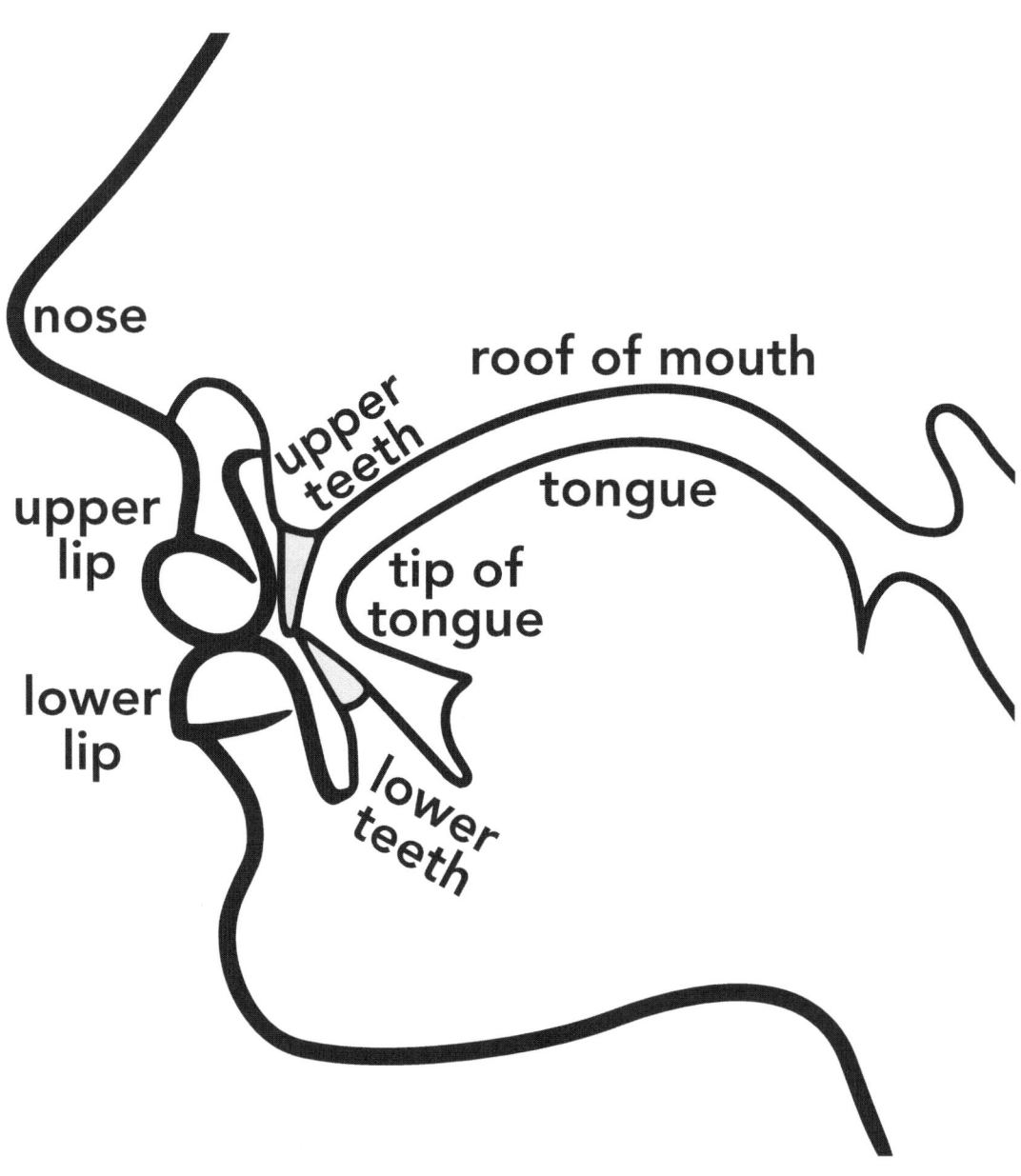

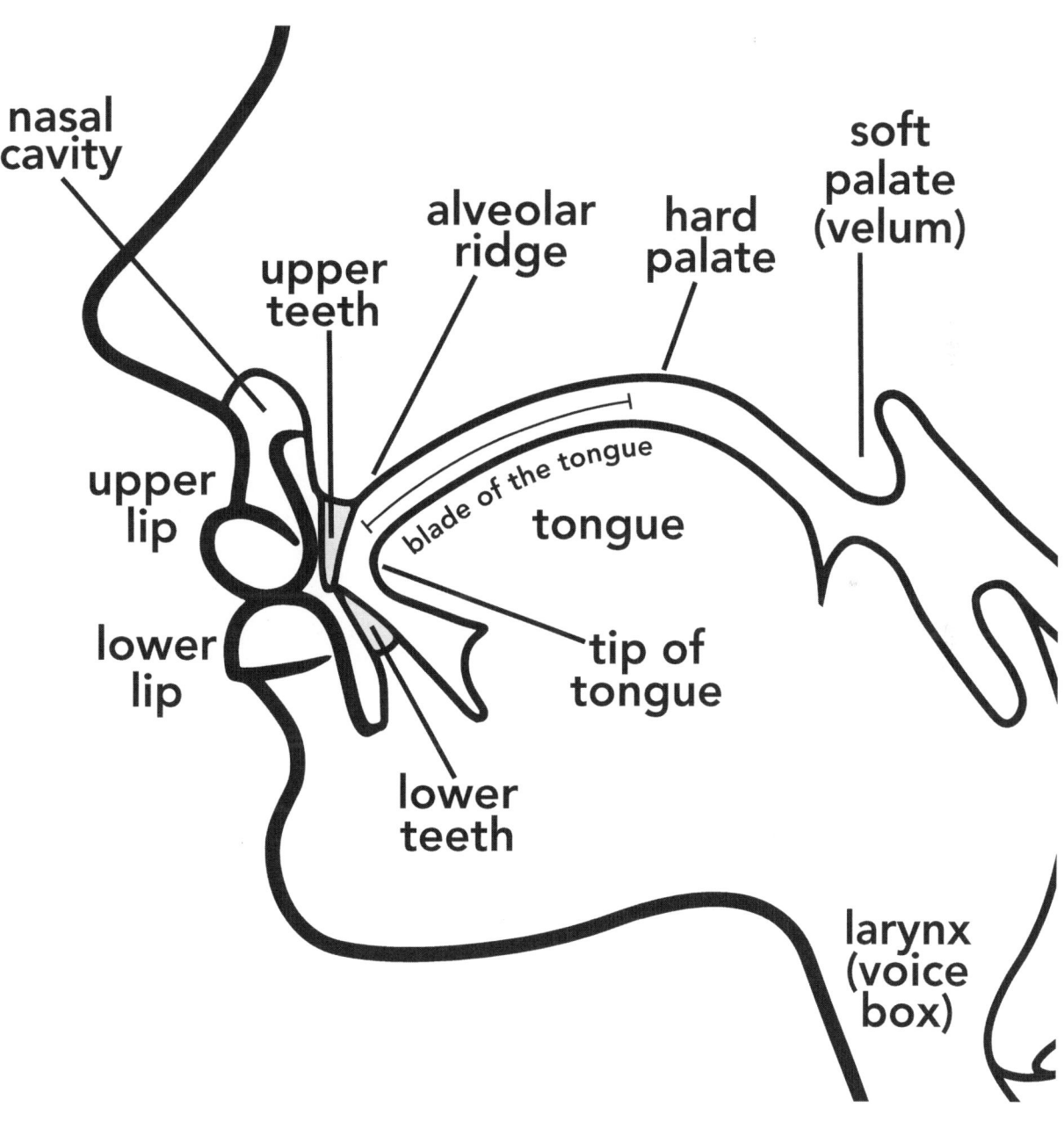

ETpedia: Pronunciation © Pavilion Publishing and Media Ltd and its licensors 2022.

1.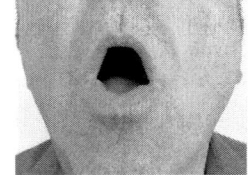

2.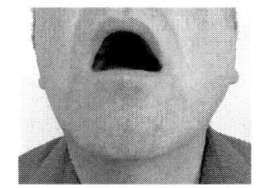

    A   B

3.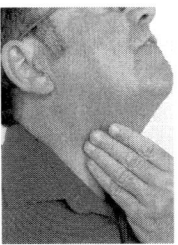

4.

5.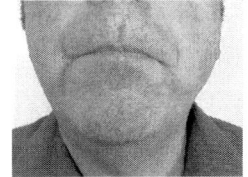

6.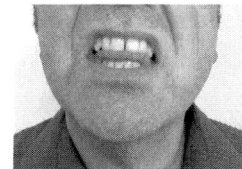

7.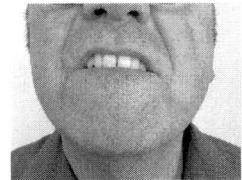

8.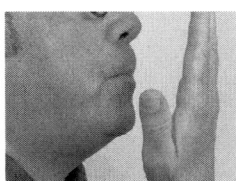

9.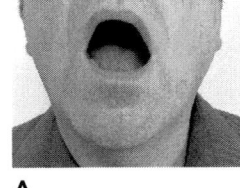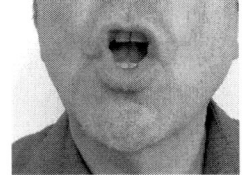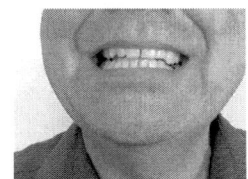

  A   B   C

You may photocopy this page.

✂

cat	tree	apple	pizza
worker	player	understand	oversee
cartoon	agree	umbrella	banana
hospital	finally	energy	beautiful
introduce	disagree	control	away

You may photocopy this page.

this	book	orange	burger
happy	sugar	understand	exercise
consistent	capital	basketball	fantastic
minimum	dependent	hesitant	energy
football	thoughtful	theatre	tennis

You may photocopy this page.

 Appendix

fish	chicken	beef	prawns
lamb	duck	broccoli	cabbage
spinach	cauliflower	onion	potato
living room	dining room	kitchen	bedroom
bathroom	balcony	sofa	television
armchair	bookcase	refrigerator	cupboard

You may photocopy this page.

••••●• discrimination	••••●• globalisation	•●••• dependency
••••●• population	•●••• equality	••●•• destination
●• swimming	●• Little	•● deserve
•● agree	●•• hospital	●•• beautiful
•●•• offensive	•●●• determined	••● Taiwanese
••● referee	••●• politician	•●••• political
●• running	•● defeat	•●•• computer
●•• pencil case		

You may photocopy this page.

 Appendix

Unit 15.7 Dominoes blank template

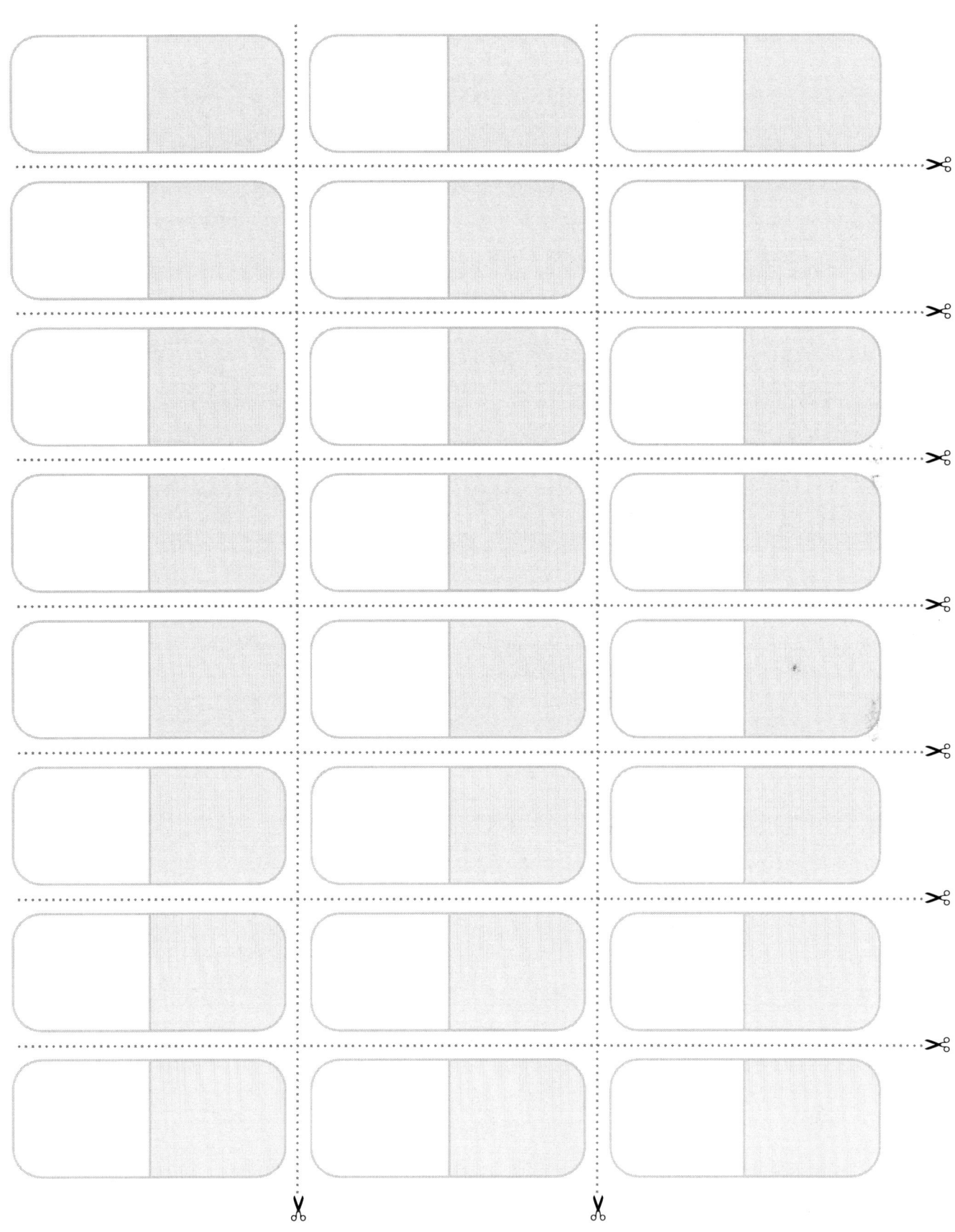

You may photocopy this page.

15.10 Word-stress table

O	Oo	oO	Ooo	ooO	oOo
sad	happy	reply	comfortable	employee	banana

First produced in *ETpedia Vocabulary*, page 182 (2019, Pavilion Publishing and Media)

You may photocopy this page.

 Appendix

18.1 British English list of phonemes

Vowels (monophthongs)		Consonants	
iː	me	p	put
ɪ	sit	b	but
ʊ	good	t	too
uː	you	d	do
e	met	tʃ	chip
ə	and (unstressed as in *rock 'n' roll*)	dʒ	just
ɜː	her	k	cup
ɔː	or	g	get
æ	cat	f	foot
ʌ	but	v	vase
ɑː	car	θ	thing
ɒ	hot	ð	this
Vowels (diphthongs)		s	sip
		z	zip
ɪə	here	ʃ	she
eɪ	ate	ʒ	vision
ʊə	pure	m	my
ɔɪ	boy	n	no
əʊ	no	ŋ	swimming
eə	air	h	how
aɪ	why	l	laugh
aʊ	house	r	read
		w	we
		j	yacht

First produced in *ETpedia*, pages 192–193 (2014, Pavilion Publishing and Media)

You may photocopy this page.

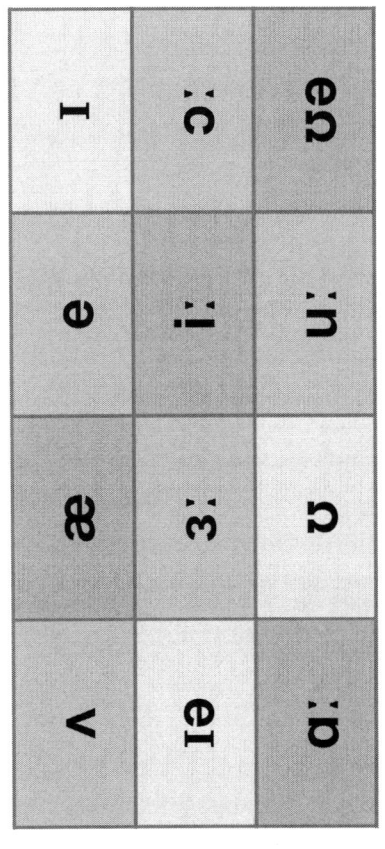

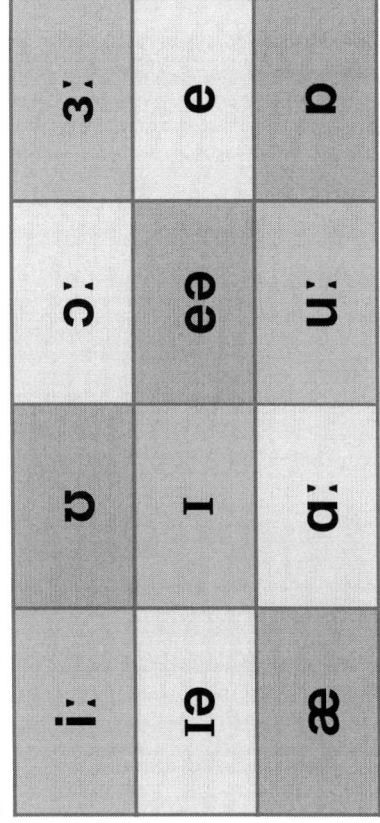

You may photocopy this page.

Appendix

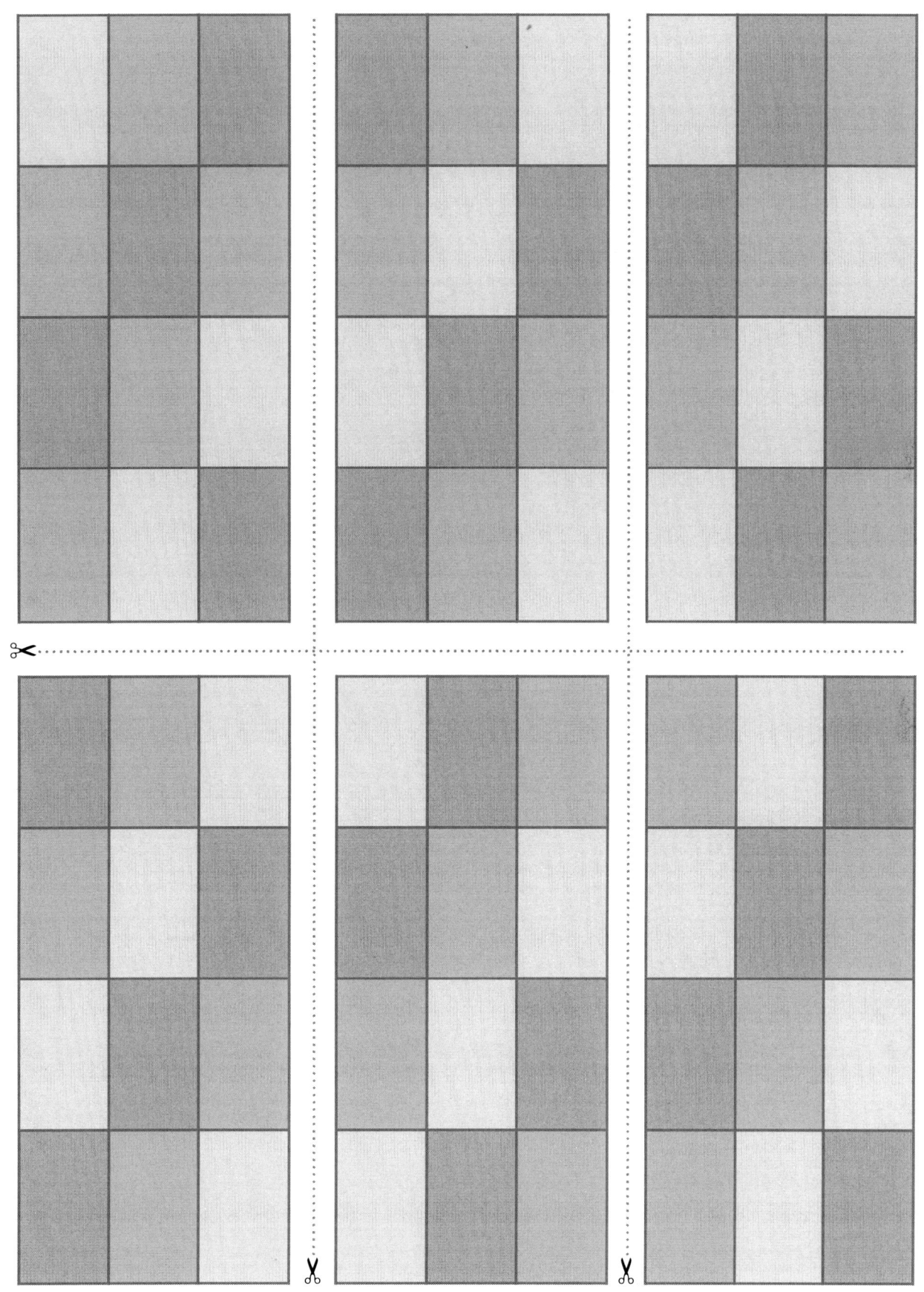

You may photocopy this page.

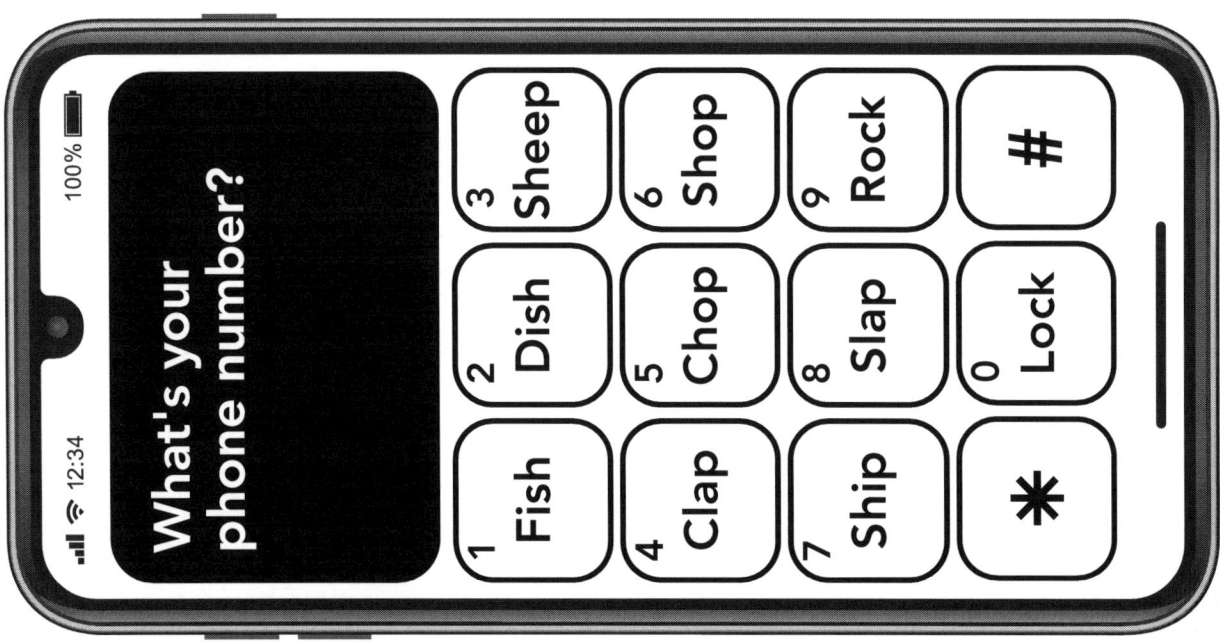

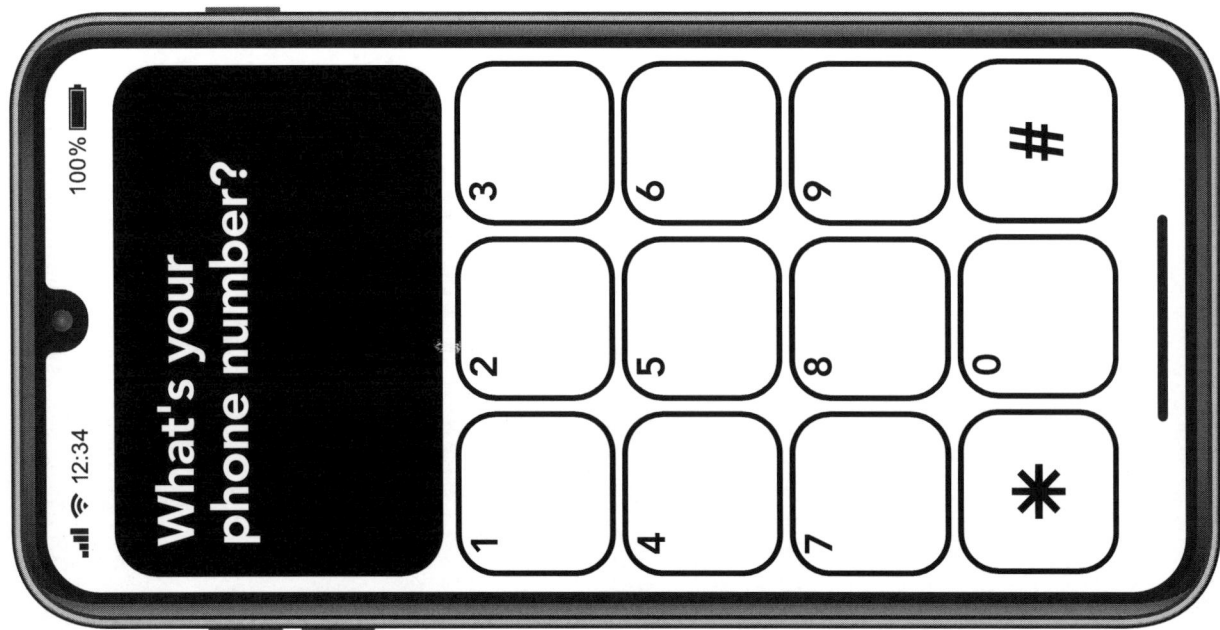

You may photocopy this page.

hit	heat	cat	Kate
ditch	dish	bed	bad
ten	den	mat	mad
three	tree	ship	sheep
pear	bear	got	cot

You may photocopy this page.

19.7 Blank pairs template

Blank Pelmanism cards for your own use.

✂ -

You may photocopy this page.

 Appendix

19.10 Phonics chart

Say the words in each row to help you remember the sounds and add your own words.

Sounds	Words with these sounds	Your words with these sounds
I	dish, symbol, this	
iː	eat, feel, three	
æ	at, cat, fat	
ɑː	barbecue, car, far	
ɒ	dot, hot, not	
ɔː	law, or, pour	
ʌ	dull, shut, up	
ʊ	book, shook, would	
uː	shoe, moon, new	
e	head, desk, said	
ə	banana, compute, hotter	
ɜː	earn, her, nurse	
ɪə	hear, here, peer	
eɪ	cake, may, neighbour	
ʊə	fewer, pure, tourist	
ɔɪ	boy, horse, voice	
əʊ	moan, phone, sewn	
eə	care, hair, where	
aɪ	bike, eye, my	
aʊ	foul, owl, towel	
p	apple, pen, up	
b	above, rabbit, stab	
t	attend, danced, tin	
d	aid, dive, played	
ʧ	chair, picture, watch	
ʤ	courgette, measure, vision	
k	baked, key, fact	

(Adapted from *ETpedia Vocabulary*, page 237 (2019, Pavilion Publishing and Media)

You may photocopy this page.

22.9 Phrasal verbs noughts and crosses

blow up	call off	find out
hold up	put away	make up
look up	set up	hand in

✂ ···

Blank noughts and crosses grid for your own use.

You may photocopy this page.

 Appendix

From 1 to 5.

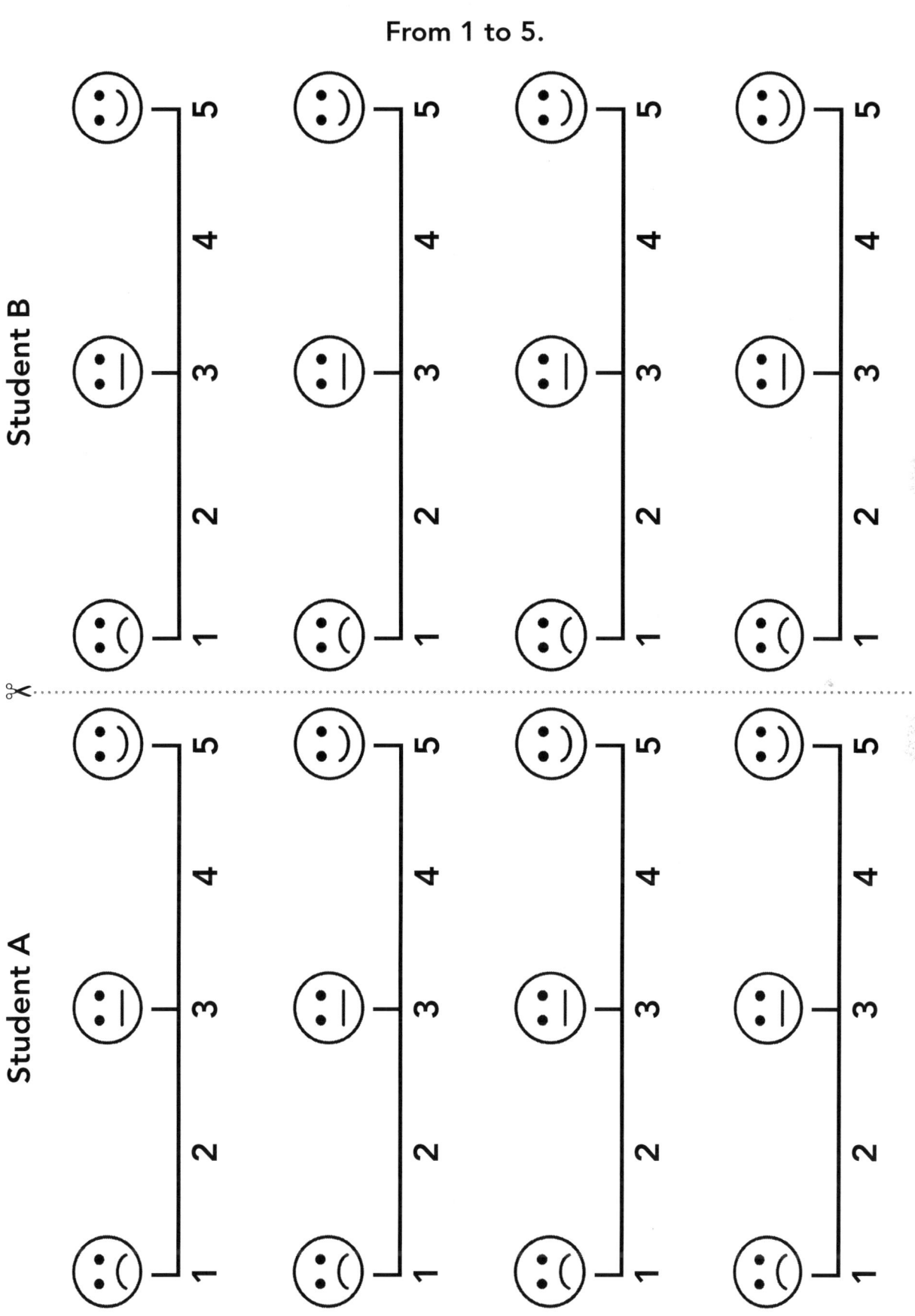

You may photocopy this page.

ETpedia: Pronunciation © Pavilion Publishing and Media Ltd and its licensors 2022.

Organising your vocabulary notebook

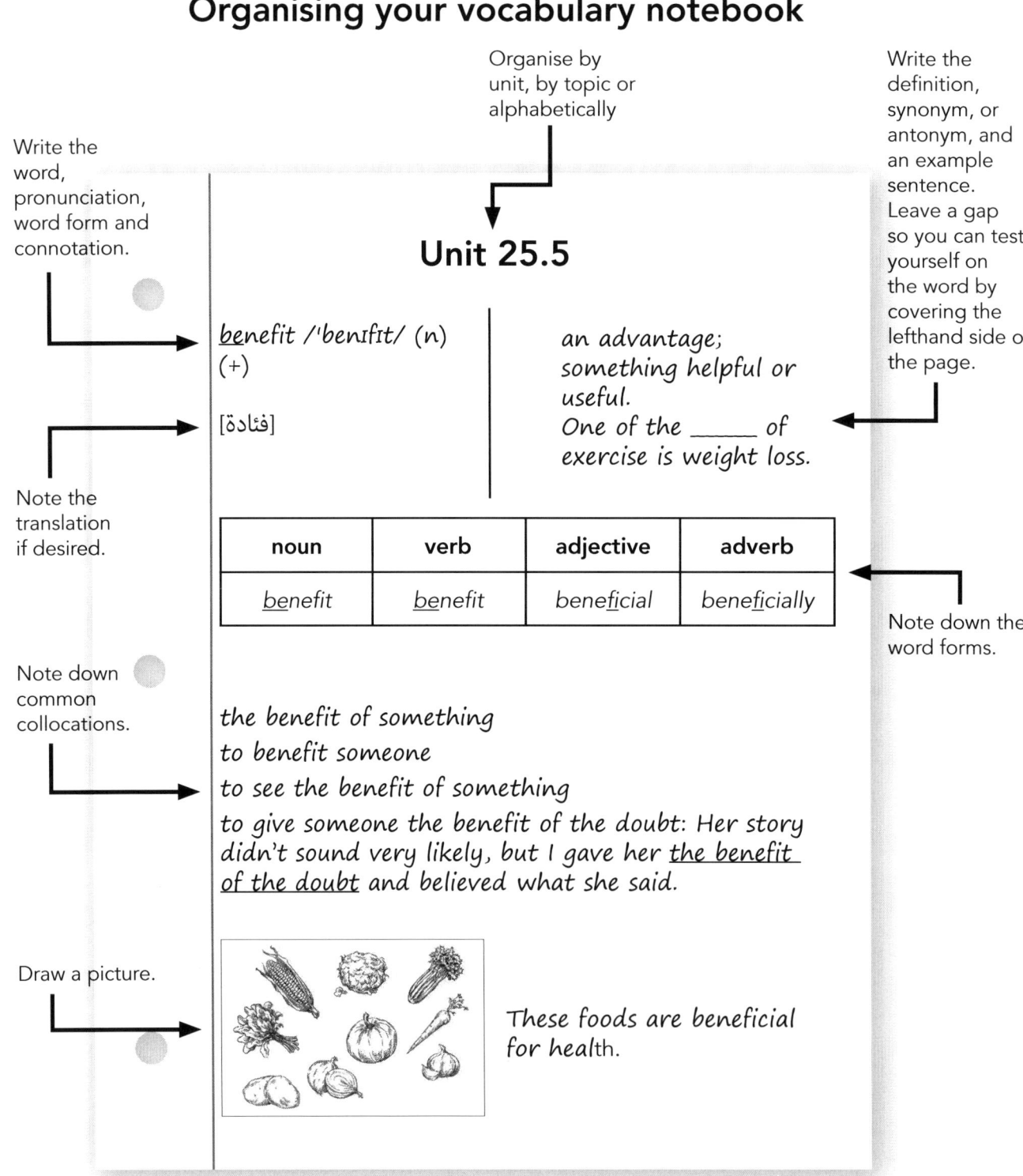

Organise by unit, by topic or alphabetically

Write the definition, synonym, or antonym, and an example sentence. Leave a gap so you can test yourself on the word by covering the lefthand side of the page.

Write the word, pronunciation, word form and connotation.

Note the translation if desired.

Unit 25.5

benefit /'benɪfɪt/ (n)
(+)

[فئادة]

an advantage; something helpful or useful.
One of the _____ of exercise is weight loss.

noun	verb	adjective	adverb
benefit	benefit	beneficial	beneficially

Note down the word forms.

Note down common collocations.

the benefit of something
to benefit someone
to see the benefit of something
to give someone the benefit of the doubt: Her story didn't sound very likely, but I gave her the benefit of the doubt and believed what she said.

Draw a picture.

These foods are beneficial for health.

First produced in *ETpedia Vocabulary*, page 187 (2019, Pavilion Publishing and Media)

You may photocopy this page.

 Appendix

Unit 26.5 Irregular verb list

Infinitive	Past simple	Past participle
bring	brought	brought
build	built	built
buy	bought	bought
come	came	come
cost	cost	cost
do	did	done
drink	drank	drunk
find	found	found
get	got	got
go	went	gone
grow	grew	grown
hear	heard	heard
know	knew	known
let	let	let
meet	met	met
read	read	read
see	saw	seen
spend	spent	spent
swim	swam	swum
teach	taught	taught
wear	wore	worn

You may photocopy this page.

Unit 26.8 Past participles crossword

Stundent B

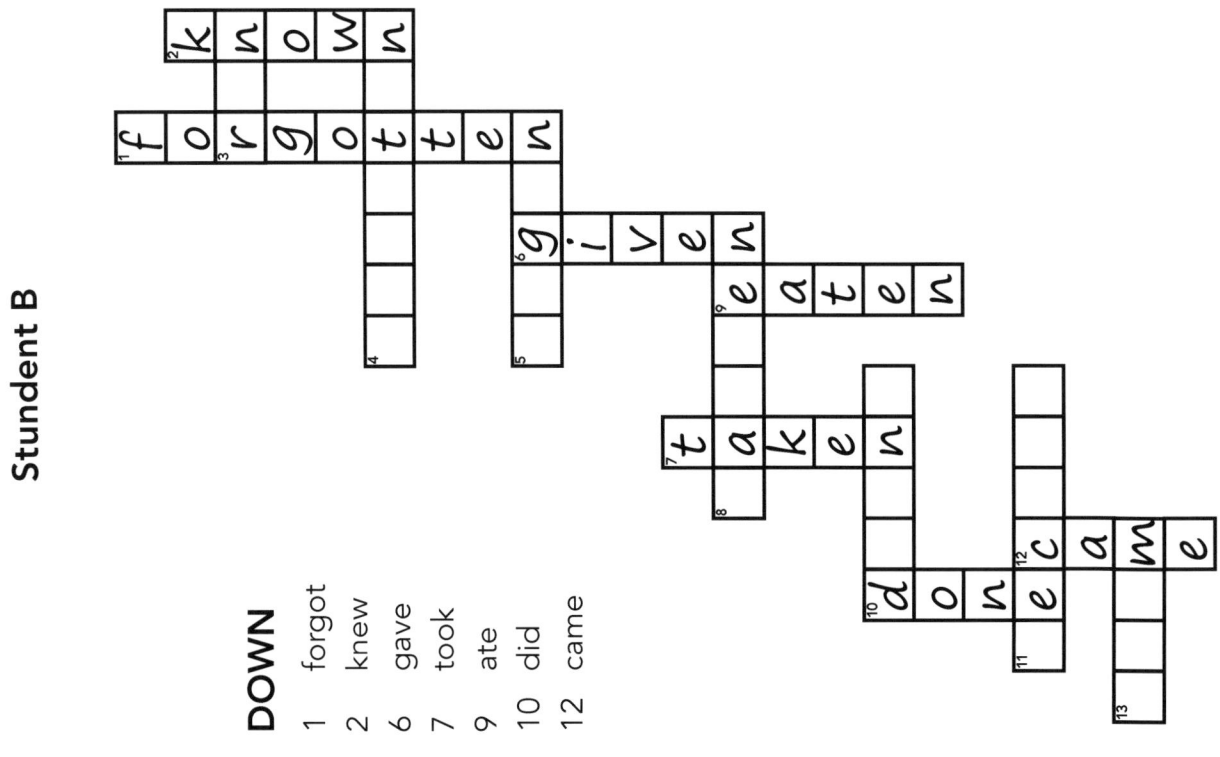

DOWN

1 forgot
2 knew
6 gave
7 took
9 ate
10 did
12 came

Stundent A

ACROSS

3 ran
4 wrote
5 begun
8 fell
10 drank
11 became
13 swim

You may photocopy this page.

 Appendix

Unit 29.5 Numbers

Match the numbers to the ways of saying them.

1.	13%	a) One point three
2.	1.3	b) One and a third
3.	$1.30	c) Thirteen degrees centigrade
4.	1⅓	d) Two thirteenths
5.	13°C	e) One million, one hundred thousand, three hundred and thirteen.
6.	1m X 3m	f) Oh one three, one double three, double one three.
7.	²/₁₃	g) Seven plus six is thirteen
8.	013 133 113	h) Thirteen per cent
9.	7 + 6 = 13	i) One metre by three metres
10.	1,100,313	j) One dollar thirty

You may photocopy this page.

aloud	allowed	live	give
live	dive	meat	meet
would	wood	read	need
red	fed	our	hour
row	know	row	cow
their	there	right	write
wind	find	wind	tinned

You may photocopy this page.

 Appendix

32.7 Blank word-stress table

Blank word-stress table for your own use. Add word stress patterns, using O for stressed syllables and o for unstressed syllables. For example, Oo could depict _happy_; oO – _reply_; Ooo – _comfortable_; ooO – _employee_ and oOo – _banana_. (See Appendix 15.10 on page 158 for a completed version).

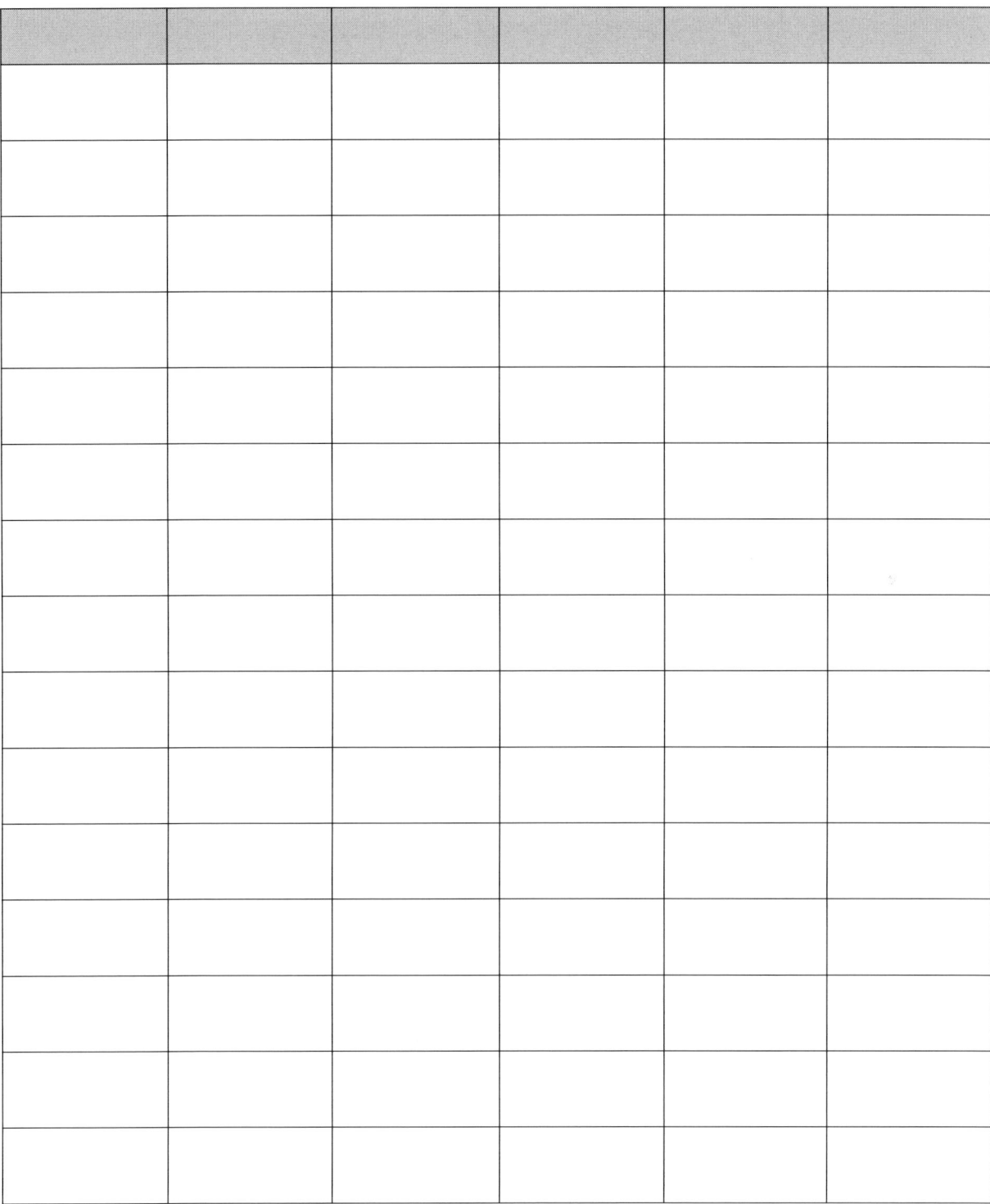

First produced in _ETpedia Vocabulary_, page 182 (2019, Pavilion Publishing and Media)

You may photocopy this page.

uː through	plough	loose	route	suit
flew	blue	group	rough	flute
sew	thought	sh<u>ou</u>lder	rude	bruise
own	Sue	do	food	bisc<u>ui</u>t
enough	**uː** threw	flood	blood	build

✂ ···

bore	bone	snore	**ɔː** nought	nor
coy	boat	law	loin	bow
ɔː court	coin	door	lawn	lot
sort	raw	through	poor	floor
south	thought	corn	mourn	flour

✂ ···

Blank maze for your own use.

You may photocopy this page.

 Appendix

1. In the table below, the two letters *A O = Can*. The letters *B X = you*. So what is this message: AO – BX – GR – KP – FZ – MW?

2. Now prepare a similar secret message for your partner. When you are ready, read the letters to your partner. Can they guess the message?

	N	O	P	Q	R	S	T	U	V	W	X	Y	Z
M	Is	she	end	black	many	Hi!	text	does	call	money	red	question	time
L	friend	long	long	train	please	nice	park	phone	plays	sport	slow	be	up
K	old	am	me	do	make	America	a	learn	use	in	lunch	famous	much
J	very	company	email	work	didn't	is	ask	class	of	who	costs	start	bus
I	fine	your	that	does	cost	would	dinner	what	don't	live	food	one	white
H	amazing	the	an	woman	are	don't	in	own	know	'd like	her	car	again
G	good	new	English	always	lend	number	go	check	sell	is	gym	bicycle	cup
F	the	where	tea	take	What's	country	meet	hello	speaks	sad	coffee	number	some
E	that	man	photo	there	are	has	first	buy	from	speak	short	breakfast	out
D	spell	surname	the	teacher	for	to	did	how	doesn't	like	two	which	Europe
C	well	bye	in	why	pizza	job	right	go	we	their	drink	lesson	age
B	I	name	nice	with	student	other	do	often	have	ever	you	hobbies	eat
A	yes	can	here	so	his	play	home	Asia	my	three	house	fast	not

You may photocopy this page.

Unit 34.10 Blank secret message grid

Instructions to the teacher: Fill the grid in with vocabulary you have been teaching recently or would like to revise. As well as adding verbs, adjectives and nouns, don't forget to add lots of other high frequency words to make full sentences such as *you*, *the*, *a*, *are*, *for*, *no*, *some* and also some questions words.

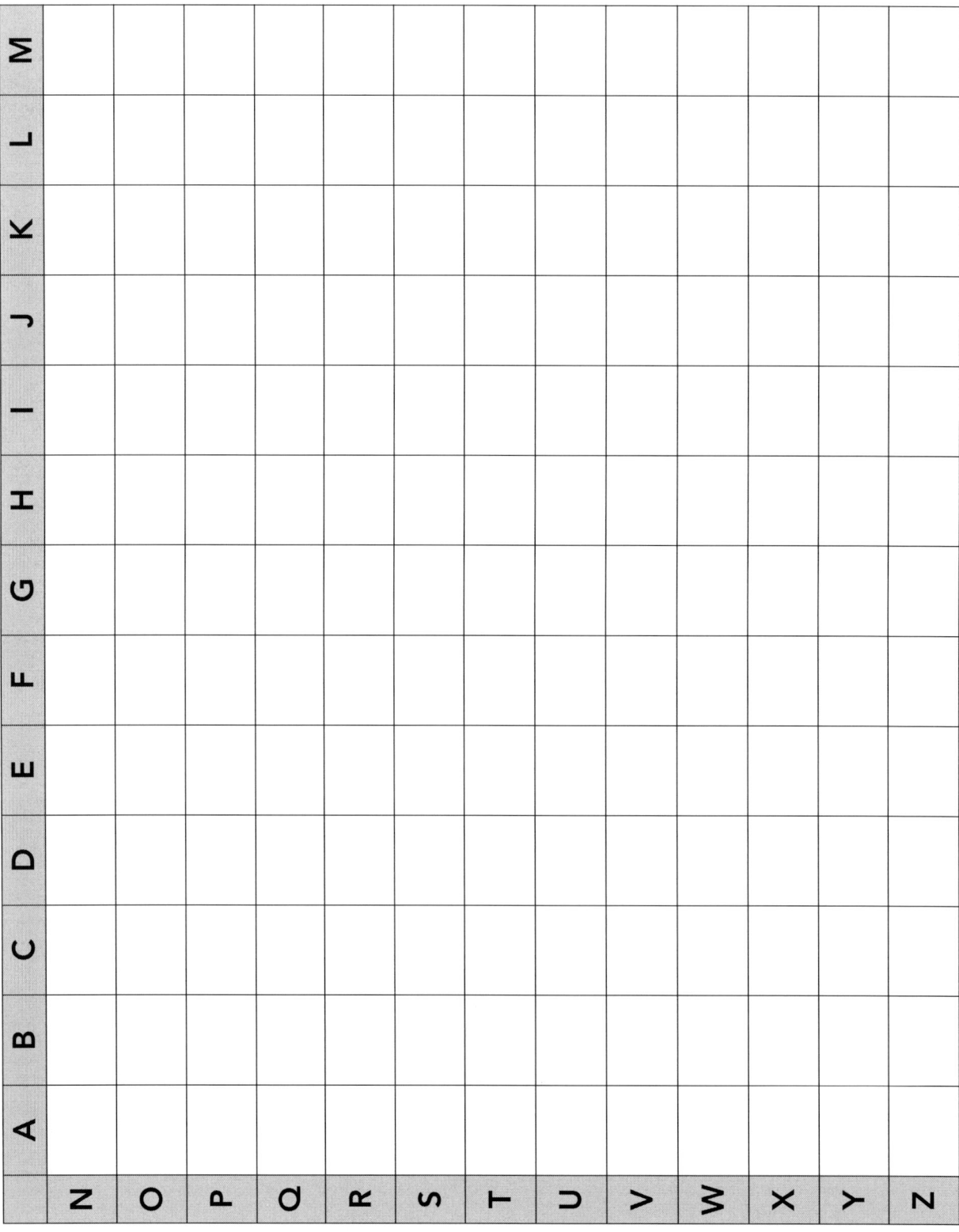

You may photocopy this page.

 Appendix

Unit 35.1 Start with an extract

STUDENT COPY

1. **Listen to your teacher reading this presentation and mark where you hear a slightly longer pause like this (//) and where you hear a shorter pause, like this (/).**
For example: / *Good morning everyone / and thanks for coming //*

Good morning everyone, and thanks for coming.

Today, I'd like to give a short presentation about a scientific process called

photosynthesis. It's the process in which the leaves of plants take the energy

from sunlight and, as a result, the plants turn carbon dioxide into oxygen.

Let's begin by looking at this slide which shows you in more detail.

2. **Listen again and underline the stressed word or words in each group of words.**
For example: / *Good morning everyone /*

✂ ··

TEACHER COPY TO READ ALOUD (and suggested answer key):

Good morning everyone / and <u>thanks</u> for coming //

<u>Today</u> / I'd like to give a <u>short</u> presentation / about a <u>scientific</u> <u>process</u> called /

<u>photosynthesis</u> // It's the <u>process</u> / in which the <u>leaves</u> of <u>plants</u> / take the <u>energy</u>

from <u>sunlight</u> / <u>and</u> / as a <u>result</u> / the plants / turn <u>carbon dioxide</u> / into <u>oxygen</u> //

Let's begin by looking at this <u>slide</u> / which <u>shows</u> you in more <u>detail</u> //

You may photocopy this page.

Appendix

START FINISH			

First produced in *ETpedia Material Writing*, page 171 (2017, Pavilion Publishing and Media)

You may photocopy this page.

 Appendix

Unit 47.9 Hidden Treasure

My treasure

	1	2	3	4	5	6	7	8
A								
B								
C								
D								
E								
F								
G								
H								

Think of words for each of your 'treasures'. Then write the word on the My Treasure grid.

Large treasure chest ☐☐☐☐☐

Small treasure chest ☐☐☐☐

Jewellery box ☐☐☐

Coin bags ☐☐

Their treasure

	1	2	3	4	5	6	7	8
A								
B								
C								
D								
E								
F								
G								
H								

Large treasure chest ☐☐☐☐☐

Small treasure chest ☐☐☐☐

Jewellery box ☐☐☐

Coin bags ☐☐

First produced in *ETpedia Material Writing*, page 182 (2017, Pavilion Publishing and Media)

You may photocopy this page.

Glossary

accent is a distinctive way of pronouncing discourse markers a language peculiar to a particular individual, location, region or nation.

articulators (or **articulators of speech**) are the parts of the vocal tract that are used in a controlled manner to shape the air that comes from the lungs, such as the tongue, lips and teeth, the alveolar ridge, the palate, the velum, and the nasal cavity.

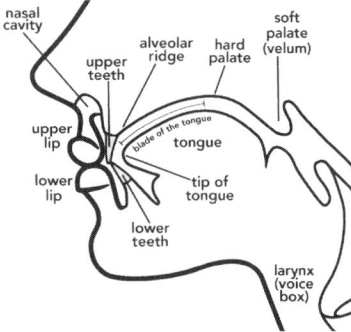

allophone a comprehensible, acceptable variant of a **phoneme** (see below).

assimilation is the blurring of sounds at **word boundaries**, meaning a sound takes the features of a neighbouring sound to link up and cause a change in sound to enable fluent speech. For instance, in *last year* the **t** becomes **tʃ** and in *cupboard*, you don't hear the two syllables *cup* and *board* separated as the **p** becomes **b** to produce **kʌbəd**.

aspiration is when sounds are pronounced with an accompanying forceful expulsion of air, such as the **h** sound in *h*at and the voiceless consonants at the beginning of words like *k*eep, *p*at, *t*op.

attitudinal approach teaches intonation by considering the **attitude** or feelings **of** the speaker, and how this affects intonation. It means that in class a teacher might ask students to listen to a speaker and decide what the emotion of the speaker might be (for instance, angry, sad, happy, distrustful, uninterested, etc.).

catenation is when the last consonant sound of the first word is linked to the vowel sound at the start of the second word. For instance, for *an apple*, listeners will hear something like **əˈnæpl**, for *pi ki tup*, they'll hear something like **ˈpɪ.kɪ.tʌp** and for *what is it*, they will hear something like **ˈwɒ.tɪ.zɪt**.

CEFR (Common Framework of Reference) is an international standard for describing language ability. It describes language ability on a six-point scale, from A1 for beginners, up to C2 for those who have mastered a language.

connected speech is when two or three sounds or words are run together as a continuous stream that they sound like one word. The main features of connected speech are **assimilation**, **catenation**, **elision**, **intrusion** and **liaison** (also known as **linking**) let someone to speak fluently and effortlessly.

consonant sounds (for example, **ʃ** as in the first letter of the word <u>sh</u>e) which are formed when the mouth restricts the air flow in some way (for instance, using **articulators** like the lips or the tongue).

consonant blend the spoken form of **consonant cluster** (see below)

consonant cluster a group of consonants next to each other with no vowel in a word, e.g. *-fth* in *fifth* or *-sps* in *crisps*. Cluster strictly speaking refers to the written form, however, many teachers use the term consonant cluster (not blend) to refer to both the written and spoken form

contractions are very common in English and happen mostly with a pronoun and an auxiliary verb, for instance, *they are* ➜ *they're* or an auxiliary verb and *not* like *is not* ➜ *isn't*. Contractions are so common in English that they are also a formalised part of written English and are indicated by an apostrophe.

contrastive stress is the way in which a speaker emphasises a word or phase in a sentence to highlight (or contrast) the difference between two ideas, for instance, <u>She's</u> *not my* **sister**, *she's my* **mother**! or *I said I wanted* **sparkling** *water!* (as opposed to the still water you've given me).

content words occur in **stress-timed languages** and are the words that carry the main meaning and are stressed in a sentence.

dark l occurs when the sound **l** appears at the end of a word, such as *ball* and *able*, or at the end of a syllable, in words like *pill*ow or *tel*evision. It can be transcribed as **l** or **ł**. The dark **l** can be difficult to pronounce correctly because of the tongue positioning, which starts out similar to the light **l** (see below) with the tip of the tongue up behind the top front teeth but doesn't pass through the front teeth (like the light **l** does), and the tongue is pulled back into the mouth. The back of the tongue lifts up slightly towards the soft palate as the sound is created, and is voiced.

digraphs are common combinations of letters producing certain sounds; for example, the spelling combination of '*ph*' often has the sound **f**.

dialogue is a written or spoken conversational exchange between two or more people, and an educational form that depicts such an exchange and can highlight features of pronunciation.

dictation is when a teacher (or sometimes a student) says a word, phrase or sentence at normal speed and the students write down what they hear.

diphthong is a vowel sound (**phoneme**) that is produced when the mouth changes while it makes the sound, moving from one vowel sound to another; for example, **ɪə** as in *d*ᵉᵃ*r*.

discoursal approach teaches intonation using the context of the sentence and is descriptive of what happens. For example, the teacher would highlight the intonation pattern of fall-rise and explain that because the speaker has already discussed the person's arrival, they are now checking the information:

What time does he arrive?

discourse markers in listening texts are what make speech cohesive, organising what is being said. So, it is important that students can identify phrases and chunks such as *first of all, as I said earlier, I'll end by …*, etc. Noticeably, these kinds of phrases have fewer stressed words and therefore contain weak forms and features of connected speech.

drill is when the teacher (or an audio recording) models the pronunciation (such as **minimal pairs**, **word stress** or features of **connected speech**) and then the learners repeat what they hear.

elision is when one or more phonemes is dropped (or elided) at word boundaries (usually the last phoneme of a word) to enable fluent speech, and reduce the time and effort it would take to change mouth position from the last phoneme of the preceding word and the first phoneme of the subsequent word. For instance: *must go* becomes *mus'go*, *stand by* becomes *stan'by* and *last night* becomes *las'night*

emphatic stress 1. is the way in which a speaker emphasises a word or phrase to affect the meaning, such as *I'm **so** tired!* (I'm not just tired I'm completely exhausted) **2.** can be used to introduce new information, such as *Sally bought the **flowers** for Jane* (as opposed to the chocolate Jane was given).

English as a lingua franca (ELF) (also known as **English as an international language (EIL)**) is a standard of English where intelligibility is the priority for English speakers, rather than an attempt to imitate native speakers of a so-called **Standard English** such as British English. The English used is a means of communication used globally and not 'owned' by one or two nations.

error is an unintended deviation from pronunciation rules made by an L2 speaker and tend to result from their lack of knowledge about the nuances of a particular pronunciation feature, grammar or vocabulary. Correcting students on the spot works best when the error is one that a student will recognise and have the ability to change. For example, if a student says 'sill' but you think that they may mean 'seal', you can repeat their pronunciation followed by the alternative, like this: 'Sill or seal?' In this way, the student hears both words and notices the difference between them. Then they choose the word they mean and try to say it again.

first language (L1) is the first language or dialect that a person has been exposed to from birth or within a critical period.

functions of intonation there are four commonly used terms to describe the functions of intonation: **1. attitudinal** (to convey attitudes, emotions and feelings); **2. accentual** (emphasis of contain-bearing words in an utterance to get the speaker's message across as effectively as possible); **3. grammatical** (a change in pitch, such as a fall or rise to signal a grammatical function such as asking a question or making a statement and pausing after phrases, clauses and sentences); **4. discoursal** (a speaker's subconscious choice of intonation patterns and tones linked to a particular speech act, or discourse, and is a product of the participants' shared histories and their shared understanding at that moment in time).

glide where the pitch of a speaker's voice rises or falls gradually rather than jumping up or down.

Global Englishes is the umbrella term covering the concept of **World Englishes**, **World English** as a **lingua franca** and **English as an International Language**.

glottal stop where a speaker closes the vocal folds and obstructs the airflow before releasing it suddenly, as may occur with words such as *but, cat*, and *bottle* – it's realised as **ʔ** in the IPA chart (International Phonetic Association chart).

grammatical approach teaches intonation in the context of different aspects of grammar and is prescriptive. For example, we might teach students that with *wh-* questions, the intonation will often fall at the end:

What time does he arrive? … whereas with yes/no questions, the intonation often rises, like this:

Are these your bags?

head (or **onset syllable**) is the second most prominent syllable in a **tone unit**, for instance, the *Can* in <u>*Can* you *help me?*</u>. This is where the **pitch** starts rising; it rises all the way to the **nucleus** (*help*). This pitch is sometimes referred to as the **key**.

homophones literally 'same sound'; also used to describe words that sound the same as another word (and are pronounced the same way) but which have a different spelling and a different meaning, such as *know* and *no*, or *bear* and *bare*.

homographs have the same spelling but are pronounced differently, so the word close in these two sentences is pronounced in two different ways: *I'm very close to my brother. / Can you close the door?* Other common examples of homographs are *lead, live, minute, read, refuse, row, tear, use* and *wind*.

intelligibility the ability to communicate with other speakers of English confidently and effectively.

International English (as used here) English produced by L2 speakers.

intonation refers to the way the pitch changes when you say a phrase or sentence, in other words the jumps, falls and glides in pitch of a speaker's voice. For instance, the pitch might rise to indicate that you are asking a question or that you are suggesting that there is more information to follow.

intonation patterns there are four main intonation patterns of English: rise, fall, rise-fall and fall-rise. In teaching, we are most interested in the intonation pattern that takes place on the **nucleus**, where the biggest **pitch** variation takes place.

intrusion is when a consonant sound is introduced (it intrudes) to bridge the edges with vowels as beginning and ending sounds to enable fluent speech. For instance, the intrusive **j** sound in *I*[(y)] *always*, the intrusive **w** in *go*[(w)] *away* and the intrusive **r** in *law*[(r)] *and order*.

inversion is when speakers switch (or reverse/inverse) the normal position of consonants in a **consonant cluster** and inadvertently change the meaning of the word. For example, with the consonant cluster **ks** and **sk** in words like *tax* and *task* or *axe* and *ask*, there would be a considerable difference if a manager was told to *axe him* when the speaker meant them to *ask* him something.

learner-centred activities are ones that are directed or led by the students as opposed to the teacher. In other words, the students and teacher share the focus and instead of listening to the teacher exclusively (see **teacher-centred** below), they interact equally, group work, collaboration and thinking for themselves is encouraged.

light l occurs at the beginning of a word, like *love* and *look*, or at the beginning of a syllable, such as *elongate* and *release*. It is transcribed as **l**. To make the light **l** the tip of the tongue goes behind the front teeth, at the **alveolar ridge** or it can also come out past the front teeth. The tongue should be in a narrow shape to allow the airflow to travel around the sides of the tongue. The tongue retracts back into the mouth, and the back of the tongue drops low into the mouth. The light **l** may feel like it is being made towards the front of the mouth.

lingua franca a language which makes communication possible between groups of people who do not share a common language.

linking (also known as **liaison**) is when the sound at the end of one word runs into the sound at the start of the next word, usually for a smoother and faster pronunciation, for instance, *runs‿into, start‿of.*

linking r often occurs when a word ends with the letter *r* and the next word starts with one, for instance *four animals* becomes 'four‿r‿animals'. This contrasts with when you say a word that ends in *r* in isolation, like *four*, where the final *r* is not heard in most accents of English (see **rhotic r** below).

L1 our first language, also known as our mother tongue.

L1 interference if certain sounds or features of pronunciation of English exist or do not exist in a learner's first language (L1), the pronunciation and recognition of particular phonemes or features might be problematic for those learners.

L2 a second or additional language.

model using your own voice (or recorded material) to introduce a new sound or word for your learners to hear and then potentially recreate.

monophthong is a vowel sound (**phoneme**) where the mouth does not change when producing them; for example, **iː** as in *tea*.

manner of articulation is the way in which the mouth makes the sound. It may involve friction between the upper teeth and lower lip; for instance, **f** as in *four*.

mistake is an action, decision, or judgment that produces an unwanted or unintentional result and can be a deviation from normal accuracy. It is done accidentally – the speaker knows it's incorrect, but the wrong word or sound slips out. The speaker can learn from their mistakes by reviewing what went wrong and identifying what they need to do to avoid repeating it. For example, if they are making a mistake like *I like at* instead of *I like art* and they're familiar with the **phonemic symbols**, draw one like this **æ** and another like this **ɑː** on the board, then point out the difference being sure to clarify which is the correct version.

non-rhotic an accent in which the **r** sound is not pronounced before consonants and at the end of words not followed by a vowel, like *part* and *far* in standard British English are pronounced as **pɑːt** and **fɑːr** by speakers with a rhotic accent.

partial assimilation is when the phoneme changes to another phoneme but a different phoneme from the one next to it. For example, at speed, *can play* will sound like *cam play*. The **n** changes to a **m** sound due to bilabial **p** that follows it.

phonetics is the study of human sounds; the production, transmission and reception of sound.

phoneme (also known as a **phonological unit**) is a distinct and single unit of **sound** in a specific language, such as English, that can distinguish one word from another, for instance **b**, **k**, **ʧ**, **m** in the English words *bat, cat, chat, matt*. English has 44 phonemes which are separated into 24 **consonant** sounds and 20 **vowel** sounds.

phonemic script language written by a representation of each of its sounds (**phonemic symbols**), rather than its alphabetical letters, specific to the language it's representing. The British English phonemic script is different to the General American phonemic script for instance, with a number of sounds looking quite different and even common words being **transcribed** in different ways. Take the word *hot* – in British English it is transcribed as **hɒt** but in American English it is shown with a longer vowel sound **hɑt**.

phonemic chart showing the 44 phonemic symbols and the way they relate to each other. Arguably, one of the most influential is the chart created by Adrian Underhill in *Sound Foundations* (1994, Macmillan Education), which is divided into monophthongs, diphthongs and consonant sounds.

Glossary

phonology is a branch of linguistics that studies and classifies the sounds, their distribution and patterns that occur within different languages and dialects.

pitch the level someone speaks at (technically the frequency). Every speaker has a normal pitch range, which they may depart from in certain situations, such as when they are excited or angry.

plosive English has six plosive consonants: **p**, **t**, **k** and **b**, **d**, **g** which follow certain patterns depending on their position in a word: initial, medial and final.

polysyllabic containing two or more syllables.

place of articulation is the position the mouth forms to produce a different phoneme, for example, the place where the upper teeth meet the lower lip.

pre-head refers to any syllables that come before the **head**. So in this tone unit: *I was <u>wondering</u> if you could <u>help</u> me? I was* is the pre-head and *wondering* is the head.

primary stress the syllable in a polysyllabic word which is given the most emphasis by the speaker, for instance, *im'portant* and *'delegate.*

proclaiming tone a falling tone used when giving information that is perceived to be new to the listener.

productive pronunciation is where learners need to produce the phonological features or sounds you have taught them.

prominence the four ways in which a speaker emphasises key words in an utterance in order to convey their meaning: by changing the pitch of the stressed syllable (pitch), by making the stressed syllable longer (length), by making the stressed syllable louder (volume) and/or by articulating the vowel sound of the stressed syllable more clearly (quality).

pronunciation refers to the way we say words.

pronunciation model is the standardised model used in a particular coursebook or course material and is often determined by where the material is being produced or published. For instance, a coursebook published by a British publisher is likely to offer a British English **pronunciation** and **phonemic symbols** as opposed to using General American pronunciation and accompanying phonemic symbols.

receptive pronunciation is where learners need to be able to recognise the phonological feature or sounds being spoken.

reduced forms words which are less clearly articulated in a stream of speech.

referring tone a falling-rising tone used when referring to something or someone that the listener is believed to already know.

register the style of language used in formal/informal situations.

resyllabification occurs when a consonant becomes attached to a vowel sound in a different syllable like *an apple* ➔ *a napple* (also known as **catenation**) and taller (with the **l** sound moving to the *er* but this is not **catenation**).

retroflex is when the tongue is curled backwards at the start of the sound, for instance the 'r' sound in Mandarin and Cantonese. When Chinese characters are transcribed into the Roman alphabet, the sound is written as 'r' but it is pronounced significantly differently from the **r** phoneme we produce in English which can lead to **L1 interference** and the belief the sounds are produced similarly, when in fact, they are not.

rhotic r is heard when someone has an accent or dialect in English in which an **r** sound is retained before consonants, such as *hard* and *market* which sound like **ha:rd** and **ma:rkɪt**, and at the end of a word like car and four which sound like **ha:ʳ** and **fɔ:ʳ** The presence of the **rhotic r** tends to provides an instant recognition of the regional speech of a given speaker.

rhythm a strong, regular pattern (or beat) of sounds or utterances in speech. For example, if you count out three regular beats and repeat the sentence *It was a hot day* a few times, you'll notice that the words *It was a* take up one beat, *hot* another beat, and *day* the final beat.

schwa represented by the phoneme **ə** is the most common sound in English, and represents unstressed vowel sounds in an utterance. For instance, *It was a hot day* is commonly said like this **'ɪt wəzə 'hɒt 'deɪ** with the unstressed words being *was* and *a* that might be barely heard.

secondary stress 1. may be found in a **polysyllabic** word where the syllable carrying secondary stress is emphasised more than the other unstressed syllables in a word, but not as much as the syllable carrying the primary stress. For example, consider the word *delegate*: in the verb, **'delə‚geɪt**, the final syllable has secondary stress, but in the noun, **'deləgət**, the final syllable is unstressed. **2**. is the word that doesn't carry the main stress in a sentence or chunk, but that is still stressed to some extent. For example, in the sentence *He bought a new laptop*, ***lap**top* carries the main stress, and *bought* carries the secondary stress.

segmental refers to the sounds (**phonemes**) that words consist of.

segmental features are isolated segments, such as the phonemes in a word.

sentence stress is the pattern of stressed and unstressed words within a sentence, with this emphasis is on words that carry important information normally, although this can change significantly, depending on the specific meaning the speaker wants to communicate – see **contrastive stress**, **emphatic stress** and **shifting stress**.

shifting stress is when the main stress in a sentence is moved (or 'shifted') in order draw attention to a different part of the sentence and its meaning, for instance, emphasise the object of the sentence by stressing it: *I flew to PARIS*, or emphasise what you were doing by stressing the verb: *I FLEW to Paris*.

slip is a mistake that the student wouldn't normally make, so it doesn't need attention.

Standard English refers to the version of English you might provide as a model, such as British English or American English.

stress is a key component of connected speech. If you listen to a sentence like *It was a hot day*, you'll notice that the two words *hot* and *day* are emphasised (stressed) with a change of **tone**. The words *it was a*, on the other hand, are not stressed, to the point that we might barely hear them, and the vowel sounds in the words *was* and *a* are likely to be unstressed.

stress pattern shows where the primary and secondary/unstressed syllables are in a word, for instance, *comPUter*.

stressed syllable of the stressed word when you are talking about sentence stress, it's easier to talk about which word is stressed in the sentence, however, it's the syllable of the stressed word, to be precise. For instance, in the sentence *I flew to **E**gypt*, the word *Egypt* contains two syllables, so it is just first syllable that is stressed.

stressed-timed language is a theory of language which states that certain words are stressed more than others in speech; the stressed words are generally those that carry the main meaning of the sentence. English is a good example of a stressed-timed language.

strong form a carefully articulated word resembling its citation form.

suprasegmental features go beyond single phonemes; they involve areas such as word stress.

subvocalisation the process when we read of noticing the letters and words and converting them to sounds in our head.

syllable is a unit of pronunciation having one **vowel** sound, with or without surrounding **consonants**, forming the part or whole of a word, for instance the word *it* has one syllable, whereas the word *iterative* has four syllables.

syllable-timed a theory of language where every syllable is given more or less an equal amount of stress in speech. Italian is a good example of a syllable-timed language.

tail refers to any syllables that come after the **nucleus**. So in this tone unit: *I was <u>wondering</u> if you could <u>help</u> me?* *help* is the nucleus, and *me* is the tail.

teacher-centred approach takes place inside the classroom and encourages the learners to focus completely on the teacher. In other words, the teacher talks, and the learners exclusively listen or act upon instructions from the teacher.

Glossary

tone the technical term for **pitch** changes (or **intonation patterns**): rising, falling, rising–falling, falling–rising and a level tone.

tone unit (or **intonation group**) is a basic part or chunk of language; it might be a single word consisting of more than one syllable, a phrase, a whole sentence, or even just part of a sentence. Within it, there will be one complete movement of intonation – a pitch change or a level tone.

tonic syllable (or **nucleus**) occurs in a tone unit, with one syllable always having the most stress. This stressed syllable is where the intonation will be most prominent or there's a change in **tone**. This is called the **nucleus** of the intonation group (or the **tonic syllable of the tone unit**). So in this tone unit: *I was wondering if you could help me? I was* is the **pre-head** and *wondering* is the **head**, *help* is the **nucleus**, and *me* is the **tail**.

transcribe is when words, phrases or sentences are written as they sound using the **phonemic script**.

unvoiced a term used to refer to a phoneme that is articulated (or produced) without vibration of the vocal cords, for instance, **p**, **t** and **k** sounds.

voiced a term used to refer to a phoneme that is articulated (or produced) with vibration of the vocal cords, for instance, **b**, **d** and **g** sounds.

vowel sounds (for example, **iː** as in *she*) which are formed using different **articulators** (see definition above) and with the mouth letting the air through.

weak form(s) a term commonly used to imply that there are a limited number of function words with reduced vowel sounds. In fact, every word has a strong and a weak form.

word boundaries the aural boundaries between adjacent words where **elision**, **assimilation** and **linking** may occur (see above).

word stress is when a word has more than one **syllable** and one of the syllables has a change of pitch to the others and is said with more emphasis, such as *louder* which has the word stress on the first syllable (LOUder) and *computer* which as the word stress on the second syllable (ComPUTer).

World English refers to the English language as a **lingua franca** used in business, trade, diplomacy and other spheres of global activity.

World Englishes refers to the different varieties of English, such as British English, Australian English and South African English, and English-based creoles (emerging localised or indigenised varieties of English) developed in different regions of the world and were often influenced by the UK or US, such as Singaporean English, Nigerian English and Indian English.

 Glossary

Bibliography

Cauldwell, R. (2013). *Phonology for Listening.* Birmingham: Speech in Action.

Esteves, V.R. (2016). *ETpedia Young Learners.* Hove: Pavilion Publishing and Media.

Hancock, M. (2020). *50 Tips for Teaching Pronunciation.* Cambridge: Cambridge University Press.

Jenkins, J. (2000). *The Phonology of English as a Lingua Franca.* Oxford: Oxford University Press.

Kelly, G. (2000). *How to Teach Pronunciation.* Harlow: Pearson.

Levis, J. (2018). *Intelligibility, Oral Communication and the Teaching of Pronunciation.* Cambridge: Cambridge University Press.

Marks, J. & Bowen, T. (2017). *The Book of Pronunciation.* London: Delta Publishing.

McKay, S.L. (2002). *Teaching English as an International Language – Rethinking goals and approaches.* Oxford: Oxford University Press.

Parker, R. & Graham, T. (2002). *The Phonology of English.* Seattle, Washington State: ELB Publishing.

Patsko, L. & Simpson, K. (2019). *How to Write Pronunciation Activities.* Oxford: ELT Teacher 2 Writer.

Roach, P. (2001). *English Phonetics and Phonology.* Cambridge: Cambridge University Press.

Swan, M. & Smith, B. (Eds.) (2001). *Learner English.* Cambridge: Cambridge University Press.

Underhill, A. (1994). *Sound Foundations.* Oxford: Macmillan Education.

Walker, R. (2010). T*eaching the Pronunciation of English as a Lingua Franca.* Oxford: Oxford University Press.

White, G. (1998). *Listening.* Oxford: Oxford University Press.